PRAISE FOR LAUREN & FINDING YOUR BRAND TRUE NORTH

"*Your Brand True North* flows like a river and I was able to float along with ease, whilst absorbing Lauren's words of marketing wisdom. Amazing ingredients to build a heartfelt successful brand. Absolutely riveting stuff to the core." ~ **Sandy B. Simmons,** Author, Speaker, Mentor

"Beyond valuable. Very readable and applicable book that every business owner should read and implement. Lauren's experience, knowledge, and understanding of the business journey is evident throughout. I give it six out of five stars!" ~ **Mary Wong**, CEO and Founder of Optimal Life Solutions

"It was a fantastic book. I loved all the insights and loved how you started with the story for the intro and use it as a metaphor for finding your direction. It flowed beautifully and I have to applaud you for all the hard work you've clearly put into this. I absolutely LOVE what I've read." ~ **Natasha Price,** Elite Wheelchair Racer, Author, Speaker, Founder of InvincAble

"We often hear branding experts telling stories without much else but Lauren is able to weave in the art of a process, combining it with a story and giving actionable steps for the reader to follow." ~ **Mark Hunter,** Mark of Approval Web Development

"Thank you so much Lauren, your words have changed my life!" ~ **Jo Tepest,** Business Owner

"Fabulous! I got so many ideas and achievable action steps to take me in the right direction that is my True North." ~ **Trudi Teren,** Portrait Photographer

"Lauren really knows what it takes to inspire true authentic and impactful action, a rare attribute in a world of canned marketing strategies." ~ **Erwin Maningat,** Symposium Host

"Fantastic! I'm now energised to take my business forwards with clarity and confidence." ~ **Gerrard Rollo,** Client Service Trainer

"This is so very helpful. It gets you to go an inch wide and a mile deep!" ~ **Lynda Petterwood,** Empowerment Coach

"This helped me question who, what, and where I am going and provided the answers! So easy to follow and filled with loads of content." ~ **Lalande Foote,** Face & Body Studio

"This is a great way to discover what you enjoy doing best and gain lots of tips to interact and engage better with your prospects." ~ **Noni Jenkins,** Personal Trainer

"I followed your advice and am already getting results within 24 hours. Your years of knowledge in the industry is priceless. Greatest of thanks so much." ~ **Michelle Cannan,** Life Purpose Coach

"This is so good for someone about to start a business or for someone who needs direction in their existing business." ~ **Jullianne Thind,** Franchise Owner

"This is a wonderful and inspirational way to understand what you do and what it is you do best. If you need direction, this is for you." ~ **Nyssa Berger,** Singer Songwriter

"This is fantastic! Jam-packed with content and incredible insight on building a personal brand and how to get your story out there and leverage it." ~ **Jenna Kenney,** Entrepreneur

"This was extremely relevant and gave me a chance to build my confidence. It's a great way to get clarity around your brand." ~ **Mandy White,** Real Estate Agent

"Very valuable tool for distilling who you are, what you stand for, and what your business is all about. Gave me clear definition for the direction of my business" ~ **David Freeman,** Freeman's Organic Farm

"If you are muddled about what you do this will get you started with total clarity" ~ **Vanessa O'Brien,** Pet Guardian

"Great value, lots of useful information, dynamic, holistic and totally understandable guidance to grow your brand identity" ~ **Anita Montesino,** Thyroid Specialist

"This is fantastic for those who need clarity and direction in business and those just starting to reposition themselves. Terrific introduction to developing your real and effective brand." ~ **Brian and Prue Keen,** Franchise Simply

"Be ready to think differently, stretch your thinking, and expect lots of lightbulb moments." ~ **Suzanne Ramsden**

FINDING YOUR
BRAND
TRUE
NORTH

LAUREN CLEMETT

YOUR BRAND TRUE NORTH

FINDING YOUR BRAND TRUE NORTH

HOW TO LEAD WITH
PURPOSE, DIRECTION, AND MEANING

LAUREN CLEMETT

www.YourBrandTrueNorth.com

www.YourBrandTrueNorth.com

First Edition

ISBN Hardcover: 978-0-6454986-1-5
ISBN Softcover: 978-0-6454986-0-8
ISBN Ebook: 978-0-6454986-2-2
ISBN Audiobook: 978-0-6454986-3-9

Edited, book and page design by Rodney Miles, www.RodneyMiles.com
Cover Design By Your Brand True North

WARNING

DO NOT READ THIS BOOK AT NIGHT. READERS HAVE ADVISED THAT THEY ARE STILL UP AT 2AM MAKING NOTES, BRAINS BRIMMING WITH IDEAS. THIS IS A PRACTICAL GUIDEBOOK, SO FEEL FREE TO USE A HIGHLIGHTER, WRITE NOTES, TURN DOWN THE CORNERS AND GENERALLY MAKE A MESS OF THIS BOOK WITH YOUR THOUGHTS, PLANS AND ACTION STEPS.

www.YourBrandTrueNorth.com

Some of the brand stories have been dramatized for your reading pleasure, however the facts behind the stories are based on research noted in the references.

CONTENTS

"Do not follow where the path may lead.
Go instead where there is no path and leave a trail."

~ Ralph Waldo Emerson

PROLOGUE

WE'VE BEEN WALKING all day and it's starting to get dark. The last of the sun has almost set behind the valley and the narrow path down the ridge isn't so clear anymore. I'm not 100% sure where we are, but I can't let those following me know we might be in trouble. Secretly I realise we could be lost.

The muddy track is overgrown, and dense bush covers the trail. It's been far too long since we saw a signpost and I don't recognise anything anymore. Everything looks the same and I'm sure we have been past this tree before. Now I'm really starting to worry.

What if we are miles from where we want to be?

Do we have enough rations to stay overnight in the bush?

How much water does everyone have?

What if we keep going in the dark and someone gets hurt?

Who has the medical kit?

When do I tell them we are not going home today?

How cold is it going to get tonight?

In the dimming light, a small green edge of wood catches the corner of my eye. A signpost! As we get closer to it I breathe a big sigh of relief. I read the destination and distance left to go and I know where we are. We are not lost, just temporarily misplaced. *Phew!* I know I can lead everyone to safety and I'm feeling more confident, only another 2.5 km to go.

Being a leader, especially in the bush, is not easy. As a follower you are simply along for the journey, able to wander after the leader taking in the scenery, keeping up with the pace, and making sure of your footing. But as the leader, you are the one who is supposed to know where to go, reading the signs, and making sure everyone is on track. Everyone expects you to know the path as the trusted, experienced, decision-maker.

People follow you because you know where to go, how to get there, when to rest, how long to go for, who's coming with us, what activity to do, when to go home, and what to do if we get lost.

It's the same when you are a leader in business. Others look to you for advice, security, inspiration, motivation, and above all, expertise and experience. They follow your lead, taking cues from what you say and do, noticing how you conduct yourself and the way you communicate. They want a leader to make them feel safe, to inspire them to push out of a comfort zone, to perform and deliver. They want us to be the leader they wish *they* could be.

But so often as leaders, we ourselves question our moves. We second guess our abilities, not sure of the direction to take, often overwhelmed by choice. As a leader you are meant to be confident and sure of yourself, but what happens when you start to doubt your own path? What happens when a leader suddenly questions who they are and loses their sense of direction?

When leaders get lost with no sense of purpose or direction suddenly they are not great at communicating what they want others to do. They then make poor salespeople and messy business owners. Entrepreneurs who haven't figured out their core values and lack connection with the business brand, tend to rush into things they shouldn't, lose focus, and get easily distracted.

This is why leaders need to know the meaning, direction, and purpose of their *personal* brand and how these align with the *business* brand. They have to develop a clear idea of who they are and what drives them, with a deep sense of why they do what they do.

If you are an entrepreneur, manager, organisation leader, or business owner and you want to lead with confidence, overcome imposter syndrome, and be totally fulfilled in life, you need to have a strong commitment to building your personal brand. If you can't believe in yourself or your brand purpose, why should anyone else? If you can't be sure of yourself as a leader, should you even be leading?

It is time to find your Brand True North.

LAUREN CLEMETT

YOUR BRAND TRUE NORTH

INTRODUCTION

GOING BUSH

THE 'BUSH' MEANS different things in different countries[1]. There are the forests of Europe, where you can wander amongst the bluebells[2], but in some places bears and wolves might eat you. In North America where the trees are big enough to drive through, rattlesnakes and mountain lions hide amongst the rocks.

Going bush in Australia usually means walking about in the Outback[3], where scrubby land[4] is full of things that with desert-like conditions can kill you (like venomous snakes and spiders), but you can usually see your way through it. Like the jungles in South America, the bush in New Zealand where I grew up is thick, dense, and tangled. Stray only a few feet from the path and you can quite easily get lost.

Regardless of where you are, being lost in business is a lot like being lost in the bush: You may have started out with an idea of where you wanted to go, but you're now overwhelmed and not so sure about how you are going to get there. You lack confidence and have lost track of where you are and what you should be doing to successfully create a stand-out brand that gets seen and noticed.

---

[1] "The bush" is a term mostly used in the English vernacular of Australia and New Zealand where it is largely synonymous with backwoods or hinterland, referring to a natural undeveloped area. — https://en.wikipedia.org/wiki/The_bush

[2] Flowers: usually deep violet-blue in colour, bluebells are bell-shaped with six petals and up-turned tips. These sweet-smelling flowers nod or droop to one side of the flowering stem (known as an inflorescence) and have creamy white-coloured pollen inside. —https://www.woodlandtrust.org.uk/trees-woods-and-wildlife/plants/wild-flowers/bluebell/

[3] The Outback is a remote, vast, sparsely populated area of Australia. The Outback is more remote than the bush, which includes any location outside the main urban areas. —https://en.wikipedia.org/wiki/Outback

[4] Scrubby land is rough and dry and covered with scrub. — https://www.collinsdictionary.com/us/dictionary/english/scrubby

So often in business you are head down, trudging along, getting on with things, sort of knowing what you want, but not 100 percent sure of the right direction to take. Before you know it you can't see the wood for the trees and all your marketing starts to look the same as everyone else's. Worse, if you are unaware of the risks you can get into real trouble in business the same way you can in the bush.

It's still quite hot in the mid-winter morning sun in Northern Queensland, as we near the top of the track to take a rest and enjoy the view. The lush green canopy gives way to a spectacular vista with the rainforest reaching right down to the water's edge. The clear blue sea stretches to the horizon, not a cloud in the sky. A slight breeze moves the leaves in the trees above our heads and we drink in the noise of nature all around us.

We head back down the track to the car, taking care to stick to the path. Many of the trees have names signposted and we stop to learn about the flora and fauna in this exotic rainforest area. A white sign, slightly larger than the others, catches my eye. It is covered in green mould and lichen so I lean in to read it better, but what I read makes me step back with caution, suddenly very aware of my surroundings. The sign warns of the *Australian Stinger Tree* or *Gympie-Gympie*[5] which is native to these areas. The words on the sign describe how the tree has venomous hairs filled with toxins running all over its branches and leaves, that, if disturbed, stick into the skin and inject their poison.

We take exceptional care as we complete our walk and make it back to the car without incident, but we now realise there is more than just snakes and spiders in the bush in Australia that you need to be wary of—even the trees are out to kill you!

---

[5] One of the world's most venomous plants, the Gympie-Gympie stinging tree can cause months of excruciating pain for unsuspecting humans. — https://www.australiangeographic.com.au/topics/science-environment/2009/06/gympie-gympie-once-stung-never-forgotten/

If you are surrounded by the wrong people in business you're going to get painfully stung and your reputation will suffer. Making poor decisions about who you go into business with—the staff you employ or the clients you choose—can be the most painful part of being a leader. In much the same way that brushing up against the Gympie-Gympie tree and suffering excruciating pain (which scientists have said feels like having acid poured on you whilst being electrocuted), the pain of a poor business decision can last for years.

In New Zealand the nastiest thing you can run into is the *tātarāmoa*[6] vine which is covered with tiny hooks. It's called 'bush lawyer' because it won't let go of you until it has extracted some blood. In business you can get entangled with any number of nasty situations that can cost you an arm and a leg and there are plenty of people out there who will sting you or cause your business to bleed money if you don't have a grasp of how your brand encapsulates everything you are, say, and do. If you get caught up with those who devalue your reputation, your brand will be damaged and harmed.

One of the biggest threats to business are the business owners themselves who, without a brand strategy end up doing what I call "WOFTAM marketing," or a "Waste Of Flipping Time And Money."

This is happening to leaders in business at an alarming rate[i] with half of all businesses failing in the first five years. I believe there are three main reasons why leaders are so affected by WOFTAM and why it is destroying entrepreneurial confidence and leading good people astray:

---

[6] Bush lawyer is a common name of a group of climbing blackberry plants (subgenus Micranthobatus of the genus Rubus) that are found in New Zealand, many of them rampant forest vines. The Māori language name of the plant is *tātarāmoa*. —https://en.wikipedia.org/wiki/Bush_lawyer_(plant)

WOFTAM Cause 1: Overwhelm

In 1960, John F. Kennedy said, "Effort and courage are not enough without purpose and direction," and he was right. Back then the human brain was exposed to around 500 branded messages a day.

In the 60s advertising was undergoing a revolutionary change with the Mad Men and Women of Madison Avenue[7] injecting humour, irony, and irreverence into what had been a staple of bland adverts for kitchen appliances and fast-moving consumer goods. Simplistic adverts for the VW Beetle became iconic, McDonald's and Coca-Cola targeted the new wave of teenagers who had become incredibly influential. But still, there were only a handful of traditional forms of media. Television ruled the household and radio ruled the airwaves.

Today our brains are overwhelmed with over 5,000 branded messages a day coming at us from multiple channels. Just like getting confused in that thick dense bush where I lived in New Zealand, the world is an overcrowded and noisy place where there is so much competition for people's attention. If you find it difficult to explain what you do and why people should choose you to be their leader, just imagine what it is like to be one of your prospective clients or employers who is overwhelmed with options and choice.

Standing out online is even harder if you are not clear about what makes you, you. With over 40,000 Google searches occurring every second, just like being lost in the bush where all the trees look the same and there's no way of knowing the right path to take, if your brand doesn't consistently stand out from the crowd, no one is going to see or notice you, let alone choose you.

If you struggle to clearly and quickly explain what makes you different and why someone should choose you, your service or products, you will lose people's attention very quickly. Worse, if

---

[7] A term coined in the late 1950's to describe the advertising executives of Madison Avenue. — https://www.urbandictionary.com/define.php?term=Mad+Men

you overcomplicate things, offering too much or using mixed messages, your ideal prospect's brain will totally switch off and you will never be seen.

If only there was some way to understand how to connect and engage with the right people at the right time with the right message so you could cut through all the noise and make a bigger impact.

WOFTAM Cause 2: Expectations

For some reason there is an expectation that anyone who starts a business naturally knows how to market and promote themselves and their services or products, even though few have any actual expertise in this area. According to research[ii] six out of ten business owners do their own marketing, despite the fact that over half of them say they don't have the skills, time, or knowledge to do it.

You may have taken on a leadership role in business based on your expertise and experience in a specific field—coaching, plumbing, accounting, finance, sales—or you might be part of a franchise brand or a member of an association or organisation which provides training and support, but very few entrepreneurs actually get taught about defining their own brand and what it means to be a leader who is aligned with their 'True North'.

Most entrepreneurs take too many risks and jump into every opportunity without knowing if it's taking them in the right direction because they don't have a brand to use as a 'litmus test' that keeps them on track. Leaders in the creative industries who do understand branding are often too close to their own brand to do it justice. The expectation of an entrepreneur or business leader is that they can 'do it all', but in reality, our brains aren't capable of multi-tasking and it all becomes overwhelming. Then we end up wondering how on earth we agreed to do all this stuff!

When you finally decide you can't be the best leader on your own and you need help, you outsource, and the problem gets worse. Without a brand strategy or clear path ahead, you can't properly explain what you want and suddenly you are wasting time and money again, without results.

If only you knew the basic foundations of a brand and how that gives you clarity and confidence, knowing you are choosing the best opportunities and doing the right things.

WOFTAM Cause 3: Too Easy

Like being in the bush and not knowing which path to take, there are far too many quick and easy ways to waste your time and money without you really knowing if your effort is going to pay off. Back in the 60s and even into the 90s, before the internet era, there were limited ways to promote your business and build a brand. Television, radio, press, magazines, Yellow Pages, outdoor and direct mail were the main channels and it cost money to advertise using them. The bigger and better the placement the more money you paid. If you wanted to really get results you paid an advertising agency to create the strategy, deliver the ideas, and place the media for you. And guess what? In order to get approval from the client to spend time and money on marketing, the campaign had to have a strategy, creative needed to be briefed, and the message had to be 'on-brand.'

Today you can create your own TV ads for free on YouTube, Instagram reels, and TikTok. Want a radio advert? Start a podcast or go on Clubhouse. Want a magazine? Write a blog on your own website or post an article on LinkedIn or Medium. With almost zero barrier to entry, low-cost and increasingly easy ways to market and promote your services or products, it is also incredibly easy to waste time and effort on things that don't or won't work. It is so much easier today for managers, business owners, and entrepreneurs who want to be seen as leaders to DIY their marketing, but easier doesn't necessarily mean it's better.

Humans create 2.5 *quintillion* bytes of data each day[iii], most of it without any serious consideration as to message, placement, or timing. The result is loads of content being created, lots of marketing activity, publicity, and sales promotions, which many consider to be WOFTAM. Leaders fall into the trap of undervaluing their time, wasting it on activity disassociated from their brand purpose, disconnected with their brand message, and often disastrous in delivering the consistency needed to become a trusted leader.

If only you could learn how to use a brand to align your message with your marketing, choose the right channels and create the right content that gets in front of the right customers.

That's why you are reading this book, to learn how to overcome overwhelm and avoid WOFTAM!

By finding a sense of purpose and direction for who you are and what you stand for as a leader in your space, you will create a foundation for *all* of your marketing that delivers you better ROI and helps you stand out from the crowd. You will be finding your Brand True North.

You just need two core tools to help you.

"Any intelligent fool can make things bigger and more complex... It takes a touch of genius - and a lot of courage to move in the opposite direction."

~ E.F. Schumacher

LAUREN CLEMETT

A MAP & COMPASS

YMCA CAMP ADAIR sits in the hollow of a valley, right on the edge of the 250-square-kilometre water catchment area known as the Hunua Ranges, just south of New Zealand's largest city, Auckland.

After school I jump off the old school bus and run down the long treelined driveway, my school bag banging against my back. It's hot and I dump my things onto the floor of our log cabin, bursting back out the door again headed for the creek. I run over to the wooden swing bridge and dive into the river. The brown muddy water is so cool on my skin as my sisters and our friends playfully splash each other and swim amongst the eels until the sun sets.

Mum calls us in for dinner and we settle into the evening. As the darkness surrounds us the night-time animals begin to call out. Inside the cosy-warm home with logs for walls we sit as a family watching the *Dukes of Hazard*, before being sent to bed at the end of another blissful day.

The dense bush that surrounds us has become our playground and we learn how to survive in it. We know what native plants to eat (*nikau*[8] and *supplejack*[9]), which to use for toilet paper (*rangiora*[10] or 'bushman's friend'), and which to avoid, like the bush lawyer (already mentioned!).

---

[8] Rhopalostylis sapida, commonly known as nīkau (Māori: nīkau), is a palm tree endemic to New Zealand, and the only palm native to mainland New Zealand. —https://en.wikipedia.org/wiki/Rhopalostylis_sapida

[9] any of various woody climbers having tough pliant stems — https://www.merriam-webster.com/dictionary/supplejack

[10] Rangiora: Thick papery leaves with furry undersides make rangiora the 'bushman's friend'. —https://www.treesthatcount.co.nz/native-trees/rangiora/

My dad is the Director of the YMCA Camp Adair in Hunua[11], and we have a brilliant childhood, playing games in the bush, swimming in the creeks and rivers, looking after pet lambs, riding our push (pedal) bikes, and going to the local country school. I'm also a member of the Girl Guides ("Girl Scouts" in the U.S.) and love camping and having adventures with my friends.

We know that straying off the beaten track is dangerous, and that you can put yourself and others in trouble really easily if you go 'bush crashing'. We know how dangerous it is when you are in the deep bush to start going round in circles or being out too late when it gets dark, and that you can fall down a gorge or stumble off a cliff.

In business, when you stray from your brand path and lose your sense of direction you start guessing and spending your time and money on marketing and promotion that has no strategy (WOFTAM). You can even start doing what you see others do, following them into oblivion, and before too long you have no idea what you are doing or where you are going.

Many leaders at this stage also lose confidence in their abilities as a leader. They get imposter syndrome and try to hide instead of lead. Those they lead begin to distrust them too, as they pick up on the loss of confidence, and before too long the entire organisation or business suffers.

But if you can find your direction again, with confidence in your experience, skills, and an alignment with your passion and purpose behind why you do what you do, you can become a strong, stand-out leader, worthy of being well-known, well-paid and wanted.

You just need to discover the tools to be that leader.

---

[11] Hunua . . . is a small settlement in the rural outskirts of south Auckland, New Zealand. Hunua is 14 kilometres (8.7 mi) east of Papakura, 3.6 kilometres (2.2 mi) from Hunua Falls and lies at the foot of the Hunua Ranges, from where Auckland obtains most of its water supply. The literal translation of the Māori language word is 'mountainous and sterile land'. — https://en.wikipedia.org/wiki/Hunua

It is there in the bush, at school, and in the Girl Guides that I learn the skill of orienteering[12]. For the uninitiated, this is where you have a map and compass and are given a set of coordinates to navigate yourself around a course, making sure you mark off the points you turn. The fastest around the course wins.

As much as I love the map and compass part, the running is not my favourite thing, but I do know exactly how useful the right tools are if you get lost.

Your *brand* is your compass:

- It keeps you on True North, gives you direction, purpose, and meaning.

- It helps you stay on course, even when the going gets tough.

- It helps you know what to say yes to and what to avoid.

- It gives you the ability to lead with confidence and instinct.

Your *MAP* is your Marketing Action Plan—the way you are going to build your brand awareness, find the right clients, attract perfect team members, and promote your business, selling services or products people need, want, and trust.

If you have your brand compass on True North, you can use your MAP to know exactly what to do to create marketing messages and promotions for yourself, your brand, and your business that anyone can follow.

And you need both—a MAP *and* a compass.

You see, in the bush or in business, if you have no idea what you should be doing and you have lost your direction and can't find the path, having a map on its own is of no use. After all, what does a MAP do? It simply shows you the lay of the land, where things are.

---

[12] Is a group of sports that requires navigation skills using a map and compass or GPS receiver to navigate from point to point in a range of natural environments and built environment. — https://www.guidelinesforgirlguides.org.au/activities_manual/activities/orienteering/

As a business leader you know that in order to attract customers, to be seen and noticed by the right people, and to sell your products or services, you need to know how to reach them. You already know that it's vital to be in front of your ideal customers as often as possible, surrounding them using a mix of social media, paid advertising, networking, and sales to be successful in promoting your business.

Trouble is, if you don't know what you are going to say to them when you are in front of them, what is the point of all the time, money, and effort you have just put into your marketing? And how do you know which channels are going to work best to reach them if you haven't worked out exactly who your ideal client is and how you can help them?

If you are just like every other brand out there why should they choose you when they do see your marketing?

Just like being lost in the bush and not knowing where you are, having a MAP might show you where prospects are but it doesn't tell you the right way to communicate your point of difference or the best message to use that will connect, engage, and convert them into clients. Using only a MAP is like marketing without any strategy, blindly getting out there and promoting your business, wasting huge amounts of time and money on activities that simply don't work. More WOFTAM.

The same goes for having a compass on its own when you are lost. The only thing a compass does is point north. It doesn't tell you where you are or which direction to go.

A brand, like a compass, gives you true meaning for your marketing. It helps you define the very reason you exist. It gives you direction for your passion and purpose, keeping you on your True North, doing what you are best at, doing what you love, creating impact, and being a positive influence to those around you. Having a brand compass on True North keeps you 'on-brand,' knowing you are doing things with meaning and purpose. Giving you the clarity to make decisions about your role, your business, your marketing and promotion, and enables you to

13

check that the opportunities that come your way fit with your brand direction.

But great branding on its own is not enough. Just like having a compass and no MAP, it's not enough that people know of you, they need to want to buy from you as well. They need to have the right message delivered to them in a way they want to receive it.

Brand awareness is costly and time consuming if you don't match it with specific, planned, and strategic marketing action. That's how good branding works, with total clarity of direction and a clear call to action.

So you need both to be successful as a leader in business, a brand and a marketing plan, a compass and a MAP. Useless on their own, the real magic happens when you get them working together. And, just like orienteering, when your marketing is fully aligned with your brand, success comes quickly.

A leader with a solid grasp of who they are and what they stand for naturally attracts the right people who feel engaged and understood, and who react positively to your brand culture and personality.

When a leader's personal brand is aligned with the business brand it is easy to reinforce the brand promise. The business leader can build a reputation and is worthy of the referrals that they earn. Customers are prepared to pay more because they respect the brand consistency. They are confident that yours is the leading brand in your industry.

It doesn't mean you won't ever make mistakes. Just like being deep in the bush you can be just metres from the path and be totally confused and lost. In your business it is the same. There are plenty of brands that screwed up. Some of their stories are in this book. The right path is there, you just need to have your brand compass set on True North and it will help you find your way.

It isn't going to be easy. To stand out as a true leader, you need to learn about your environment, and to understand what skills are needed in order to stay alive. Many successful brands started as a tiny idea, a small concept or a dream that they focused on, got obsessed about, and worked hard to build into the businesses and leaders they are today. Their stories are here too, and just like them, you need to understand the foundations of your brand, where you stand, and how to plan where you are going. Once you've done that, you need to stick to the track, putting one step in front of the other, staying on the path if you want to avoid WOFTAM and be the go-to leader.

It isn't going to be all downhill, either. Leaders who have reached the summit of success didn't get there by climbing down. They had to take many steps up to get where they are. You will definitely need to dig deep to answer some of the questions this process of brand building will challenge you with. At times you may feel confused or overwhelmed. Some of the questions are unlike anything you may have been asked before and it might be an uphill battle for you. But keep going, believe in yourself and find a way.

It is worth it.

If you are reading this book, feeling a bit lost in business or in your life as a leader, finding your way back to the path can take effort, focus, and commitment. But it is also incredibly rewarding, because when you find your Brand True North in business, everything begins to align.

If you are a leader and you feel a little off target, lacking direction, or you've simply lost your mojo and passion, perhaps you don't want to admit it, but it's likely you have strayed from the path of your True North and it's not so easy to see your way forward. Not knowing your True North not only leads to a lack of focus, but also a loss of self-confidence and that drive to be a leader. Without confidence, drive, and focus, chances are you will give up when the going gets tough.

I believe the worst thing you can do in life is get to the end of it and regret not doing what you loved, not being the best you could have been, or falling short of your own expectations of the leadership impact you know you are capable of having.

If you feel your business is ticking along but you have lost your sense of accomplishment or purpose, perhaps now is the right time to check that you have a brand that is on True North and that you have a Marketing Action Plan that is aligned with your brand.

I'm not a brain surgeon or psychologist, but I have worked on hundreds of personal and business brands and won awards with leaders, entrepreneurs, innovators, and business leaders who knew they had something to offer the world, but just needed the guidance from someone outside their business to help them find their way into the light of success. For all of the many years I have worked in advertising and marketing, I constantly put myself in the shoes of the consumer in order to help leaders in business develop brand identities and marketing communications that resonate and encourage consumers to act.

In this book I will share with you the *neurobranding*[13] secrets you need to get clear on your brand purpose, giving you the direction to cut through the noise with a brand promise that prospects can trust, cutting through their brains' defence systems to build brand awareness, recognition, and loyalty. The skills you will learn are usually kept within the walls of the big brand agencies, but you can apply them to your personal brand, to your business, or to help direct the marketing for a franchise brand or corporate business.

This book is very much about you, the leader. But it is also about how you relate to those following you. When deciding to trust a leader, humans come from a core emotional desire, focused 100 percent on themselves and the WIIFM—What's In It For Me?

Following the steps in this guide will help you and your brand to connect with your ideal prospects on an emotional level, communicating with the chemicals released in their brain so that instead of filtering you out and positioning you as just one of

---

[13] Neuroscience and branding, also known as *neurobranding*, applies the field of neuroscience to your business' brand. Neurobranding helps you to drive brand development, increase the effectiveness of campaigns and reduce the risks of a rebrand. Applying science to your brand means you stand out for the right reasons so your brand value increases. —https://www.think-beyond.co.uk/our-services/neuroscience/neurobranding/

many competitors, they are captivated and engaged with your marketing message.

Once you have your brand compass with your True North aligned with your purpose as a leader, you will be able to easily tell the world why you do what you do, not just what and how. You will be able to develop a brand promise with meaning and purpose that will help you explain how you are different from your competitors and why someone should choose to follow you. You will be able to create a brand culture that attracts the best people who know distinctly and agree with the way your business does things.

If you consider why people follow leaders, it comes down to three key trust factors:

1. Recognition
2. Respect
3. Reputation

In order to be seen and noticed, standing out from the crowd with a recognisable brand, you need to be well-known.

If you want to be valued, in-demand and worthy of being remunerated for being the leader in your space, you need to earn peoples respect. You need to be well-paid.

To be a trusted leader, you need a reputation as the best in business, in life, in whatever you choose to do. You need to be wanted.

1. Recognition = well-known
2. Respect = well-paid
3. Reputation = wanted

These 3Rs will help you get in the right mindset to find your path, giving you a clear idea of the summit you want to reach, so you have a goal in mind before you start to develop your brand. Before we get into finding your Brand True North, we need to see the benefits of the 3Rs of branding.

"If you do not change direction,
you may end up where you are heading."

~ Lao Tzu

THE 3RS OF BRANDING

YOU NOW KNOW the three vital factors that build a brand if you want to be a stand-out leader and become well-known, well-paid, and wanted, which are recognition, respect, and reputation. These are essential to any brand, be it a business or a leader. For if a brand is an asset for a business, making it different from others, promising something others don't, then surely it is the same for a person!

Donald Trump once said "A business without a brand is just a commodity," and that's why—if you are sick of blending in and looking like every other consultant, coach, sales agent, business owner, or entrepreneur—'branding yourself' is vital, even if you work for another business, franchise, or corporate organisation.

As a leader you are 'selling trust,' so the last thing you need is to disappear into a sea of providers who all promise the same thing. You need to have a brand that clearly communicates why someone should choose you, and you are going to have to catch people at a time when your solution is the most relevant. The problem is you never really know the exact time someone is going to say, "Right, I need to talk to an accountant," or, "I'm ready for a personal trainer or business coach now." You have to find a way to surround your prospective clients so they stop and take notice of your brand and file it into their memory, so when they want to sell their home, get their pool cleaned, set up their financial future, or improve their lives in some way, you and your brand are right at the top of their mind.

And you are going to have to do it with a brand that captures attention and captivates your audience. The average human attention span is less than a goldfish[iv]. If you have created an online brand, you need to know that over half of the people searching online will not wait six seconds[v] for a website to load. Not only are you going to have to get through all of the other 5,000 brand messages your potential client is seeing, you are going to have to engage and inspire them creating a lasting memory within milliseconds.

Then, once you have made them stop for long enough to want to know more about what you do, you are up against their internal defences. Many people refer to this as gut instinct, but it has nothing to do with our gut and everything to do with the part of our brain that likes to keep us safe.

The *amygdala*, or as Seth Godin[vi] calls it, your 'lizard brain', is a small almond-shaped piece deep inside your brain that can be defined as your 'fear centre'. Its primary role is processing memories and emotional reactions. It is an early warning detector, constantly checking our environment for anything that might do us harm. It stops us from making bad decisions and could ensure your brand is disregarded and never thought of again, if we're not careful about our branding!

As a memory bank gatekeeper, your amygdala will recall if you have had a bad experience with a brand. These bad memories will be recovered and attached to the current situation. The amygdala will start shouting at you, "Warning! You got hurt before, be careful, don't trust them, you remember what happened last time..."

It's the primary reason why none of us like to be sold to, and why no one likes selling. It's the reason selling or promoting ourselves is so difficult. Selling or being sold to makes us feel uncomfortable because the lizard brain is yelling and screaming at us to run for the hills.

So how can you get past the lizard brain defence system and become well-known, well-paid and wanted? You create a brand that does the selling for you. It positions you and your business as the leader.

Recognition

When your brand is recognised you won't have to spend time convincing anyone. If positioned properly, your brand naturally attracts the right clients and teams, the ideal partners, sponsors, or suppliers and projects expertise to work in your business. Consider the Nike tick ("Swoosh") everyone can identify even without the brand name, or McDonald's Golden Arches, where kids only need to see one hint of them to beg you to stop the car.

Your brand is more than just being recognised in the street though, it's about having a personality and brand culture you infuse into everything you do.

Strong personal brands include Richard Branson who once said "I'll try anything once," and has a reputation as 'Mr. Yes[vii]'. His brand is positive, innovative, risk-taking. The entire Virgin brand, which covers travel, health and wealth, focuses on taking care of the team, knowing they will take care of the customers. The way Richard runs his life, who he associates with, embracing his dyslexia and his fear of public speaking, focusing on the positive impact he has and the legacy he leaves, is so inspiring to many. He attracts entrepreneurs who admire and uphold these brand values for themselves.

His personal brand flows over into the entire brand culture at Virgin. When you engage with the brand, you know what to expect. It would be very odd if suddenly he started to become overtly risk-averse, having analysis paralysis, or doing things that were self-centred and negative. What if suddenly Virgin totally changed their brand, had a new approach, or a different focus?

The human brain likes what it knows and having a consistent personal brand is vital to generate a recognised and trusted brand, especially in a very cluttered space. The amygdala or fear centre of the brain relaxes when it recognises a familiar face, but kicks into high alert if something is out of place. You need to have a consistent message and a brand story that's easily re-tellable. Your brand needs to have a certain sense of familiarity that people can trust, even before they meet you.

People like what they know, they trust reliability, they naturally seek safety, even if you are a totally innovative change-maker as a leader. Consistently showing up with a recognisable brand, in person, online, in the media and other places, might be boring for you, but for your prospects, it's vital they see you to feel like they know you.

Don't worry if you feel you are repeating yourself, looking the same, sounding similar or repurposing or re-sharing the same content over and over again. You need to create recognition in order to create a tipping point, where people no longer just need your services or products, they now want *you* to provide it to them. With recognition, yours is the brand they remember and reach out to when in need.

Decide today, what do you want your brand to be instantly known and recognised for? Consider the brands you most like and trust. What recognition factors do they have?

Think about your brand personality:

- How do you look and sound?
- How you make people feel?
- What is it about your brand that people can feel they really know?
- What are some of the ways you are constantly showing up?
- Can you repeat those more often?
- Can you repurpose content? Is your online presence consistent and recognisable or are you all over the place?

Consistency is key to becoming recognised and it makes you well known.

Respect

A brand defines your 'trust currency,' and the level of respect people have for your brand correlates directly with how much they are prepared to pay for your services, products, or leadership. There are three ways to devalue your trust currency:

1. The first is to be vanilla, just like everyone else. You use images, colours, logos, messages and marketing that look like everyone else in your industry and there is no reason

why someone should choose you, let alone pay you more than others, because your brand is not giving them any reason to consider you are better than anyone else.

2. Or you can be invisible, just like wallpaper, so no one even notices you. Without a brand or online presence, using a Gmail address or failing to show up, you have no personality, no familiarity, no reason for people to find you let alone pay you to lead or help them. Yes, there are totally successful businesses that do not market or promote what they do. But these are not people who want to be known as leaders. They are happy working away in the background. They can still create impact and influence with a loyal audience and niche market.

3. The final way to quickly devalue your trust currency is to try and help everyone and to do everything. Choosing your niche, learning to say 'no' and deciding what you are really good at or want to do or be known for is not easy, but it's vital if you want to be the well-paid specialist. You can become really well-known for what you *don't* do as much as being known for what you *do*, do. We will go into this more when we go through the single-minded purpose of your brand in the section titled, "NORTH."

Trying to do and be everything is the trap most leaders fall into when they build a brand. They keep changing direction spreading themselves thin, adding more and more products or services and making lots of promises, then failing to deliver. Each time delivery is substandard or fails to hold up the brand promise, a bit more trust is destroyed and the value of the brand decreases. We are living in the age of the authentic brand and you must deliver on your brand promise.

Over-delivering is even better. Surprising and delighting your clients is the #1 best way to be valued and respected. Sticking to what you do best and staying on track, in your niche, makes you the respected leader. Aligning your brand with symbols of respect, like winning awards for what you do, adds a coat of gold to your name.

The longest serving monarch in the world, Queen Elizabeth II, has global respect and once said, "I have to be seen to be believed.[viii]" So if even the Queen has to show up and demonstrate her leadership, what can you actively do to create and generate respect for your brand?

Getting reviews, writing books, being interviewed on podcasts and video blogging are all helpful ways to earn respect. The easiest and fastest thing you can do to improve your trust currency is follow the lead of strong personal brands who are constantly giving.

I'm sitting at the back of a massive conference hall at the Brisbane Exhibition Centre. Although it's bright and sunny outside, hundreds of people have chosen to sit in a darkened hall, seated in uncomfortable plastic chairs for hours, listening to the speakers. The notebook on my lap has lots of notes and doodles. I've learnt some new ideas and concepts but I am waiting for the main act and he's up next.

The lights come up on the stage, the music blares and the MC introduces the speaker, "Please welcome, Mr. Gary Vaynerchuk![14]" The crowd goes wild, people jump to their feet, clapping and shouting as Gary steps onto the stage.

Gary begins to share his words of wisdom but one thing he says will stay with me long after the event. He asks the audience, "Why do you think I give away so much valuable advice all of the time for free? . . . Because I am building a brand".

It might feel counterintuitive, but consciously giving away your advice, tips, tools to others, speaking at events, posting helpful comments online, sharing action steps in blogs and articles, posting how-to videos, guest blogging and sharing articles in

---

[14] Gary Vaynerchuk (born Gennady Vaynerchuk; November 14, 1975 . . . is a Belarusian-American entrepreneur, author, speaker, and Internet personality. He is a co-founder of the restaurant reservation software company Resy and Empathy Wines. First known as a wine critic who expanded his family's wine business, Vaynerchuk is now more known for his work in digital marketing and social media as the chairman of New York-based communications company VaynerX, and as CEO of VaynerX subsidiary VaynerMedia. — https://en.wikipedia.org/wiki/Gary_Vaynerchuk

industry magazines are all ways your brand shows up and develops trust. When you are being of value to others, they in turn, value you.

The biggest mistake professional service providers and leaders make is they think personal branding should focus on promoting themselves rather than promoting the transformation they deliver. Let's get 100 percent clear: personal branding is not about how much you know, it's about how much you know about your ideal prospect, and how much value you can be to them.

As a leader you are expected to know what's going on inside the head of your followers. It's highly unlikely that consumer behaviour is one of the subjects you have been told you need to learn, but I highly recommend you understand why people buy.

A vital aspect of finding your Brand True North will be to understand purchasing behaviour and decision-making so you can better communicate how your brand transforms their life and what the outcome is that you deliver. This makes your brand of immense value to them.

When it comes to respect, if you want to stand out from the crowd, you need to be of the mindset that you have a niche. You need to be prepared to draw a line in the sand, highlighting all the things you won't do, knowing what you can deliver in terms of exceptional outcomes each and every time. Your focus is on creating a brand that everyone wants to work with or for.

If you want to be a respected leader you need to make earning respect the core of your brand purpose and focus on how your brand will deliver on its promises.

And remember, humans choose with emotion and justify with fact, they want to trust you before they buy you. A respected leader keeps their word, leads by example, and goes the extra mile, never leaving anyone behind.

Earning respect is how you become well-paid.

Reputation

Jeff Bezos[ix] of Amazon said, "Your personal brand is what people say about you when you're not in the room." When it comes to providing a professional service, being the leader in your industry with a never-ending stream of referrals, reputation is everything.

Word of mouth is your best form of marketing in order to become wanted as the market leader. It's free, it's third-party endorsement, and it spreads like ripples on a pond, reaching people you didn't even know existed.

For others to talk about you, you need to be clear about what you want them to say. Don't rely on assumption. You need to use words to describe yourself that can be easily remembered, recalled, and repeated.

I was once introduced to speak at an event and the MC said something along the lines of, "Lauren has dabbled in many businesses…" I was beside myself when I heard this, and very embarrassed. I never 'dabble'! My brand is the total opposite of dabbling. I commit 120 percent to everything I do. Your Brand True North is all about focus, direction and consistency. So why did this happen? Because I hadn't taken the time to give the MC my bio, to provide her with the words I wanted her to use to describe my brand.

- Have you created a brand bio that uses language and words that really encapsulate your brand?
- Do you use phrases and stories that are easy for others to remember and retell?
- What does the About page of your onlIne presence say?
- When was the last time you refreshed it?
- Are you giving people the right impression?
- And what do you say about others?

When I meet someone who is always complaining or sharing gossip about others it makes me feel uncomfortable. I wonder, *If they are saying things like that about others, what do they say about me when I'm not here?*

It is the same when you know someone has given a fake review or endorsement.

Giving recommendations and providing testimonials for others is a great way to associate your brand with other leaders. This 'branding by association' can level up your own brand, as long as you know, like, and trust them and you are being honest.

Consider the last time someone asked you for a recommendation or referral. What's your biggest fear? That the person you recommend or refer them to turns out to be not so good, right? Personal recommendations, referrals, introductions, all require the person giving them to have 100 percent confidence in the person they are talking about.

And when you want to become the best in business, you want people to refer to you for the right reasons.

- What do you want others to say about you?
- Have you given your raving fans the right words?
- Are you referring others who in turn will recommend you?

The content in the About section of your social media and on your website should explain who you help and what you do for them, providing a brand story to share. Your bio should clearly share your expertise and use everyday language that others can easily repeat. But mostly, it should be storytelling.

The brain loves a story, it's the most natural way to learn and share information. Do it well and your brand story will be retained and retold to others.

- What is your brand story?
- What is the start, the middle, and the end?

- What is the purpose of the story, like *Aesop's Fables*[15] or fairy tales with meaning?
- What lesson do you want people to learn from it?
- When you think about what you'd like to be known for, what comes to mind first?
- What are the fewest words you can use to describe yourself?
- Can you use repeatable words that rhyme or sound similar to each other?
- Think of all the great speakers you have heard or people you have met and the one thing that stuck in your mind that was so easy to retell to others long after the event. What was it about their story that is so retell-able?
- What was the *wow* factor of their story?
- Did it state a fact that made you stop and listen?
- Did they have a catchphrase, tagline, or zinger that instantly comes to mind when you think of them?

Start writing your bio as a brand story. Make sure it is relevant to what you want to be known for and make it flow like a children's story. Make it interesting, use common language, captivate, and get attention. If you can, create a *wow* factor with emotion in your story. Then cut it down into a short bio and from there, cut it down even further to a 'tweetable' short statement or phrase that can become your tagline.

Your brand fable or tale is a great way to have your brand referred to with a quick story that is totally repeatable, making it easy for others to broadcast your reputation.

---

[15] Aesop's Fables, or the Aesopica, is a collection of fables credited to Aesop, a slave and storyteller believed to have lived in ancient Greece between 620 and 564 BCE. Of diverse origins, the stories associated with his name have descended to modern times through a number of sources and continue to be reinterpreted in different verbal registers and in popular as well as artistic media. —https://en.wikipedia.org/wiki/Aesop's_Fables

NOW THAT YOU have the three Rs of branding, you are ready to take the next step to dig deeper into how a brand can create emotion and connect deeply with an audience, creating raving fans and loyal customers.

- You understand that the 'know, like, and trust,' so often referred to, is all about building recognition, respect, and reputation, in order to be well-known, well-paid and wanted.

- You have learnt that the brain interacts with brands using memory and emotion. The decision-making centre of the brain recalls how you felt last time you saw a brand, directing your attention and influencing a buying desire.

- Now you know that people buy a brand for a service, product, business or person, based on the outcome it delivers and how it makes people feel.

  You don't drink a Coke because you are thirsty, you drink it because it's a socially acceptable beverage. This is because Coca-Cola's branding, marketing message, and advertising has been constantly telling you it is fun, with images of people gathering, being sociable, being amongst friends, having a party while drinking Coke.

  Bank brands create emotions of stability and reliability in order to make customers fear change.

  Real estate brands feature happy families, excited new homeowners, and comfortable retirees.

  Insurance brands either play on the emotion of fear with images of terrible accidents or drive desire for safety with stories of safety and carefree living.

- What emotion does your brand generate?

- How do you want people to feel when they interact with your brand?

- What emotion drives people to want your brand?

- The human brain, albeit a complex mechanism, really does want things to be simple. The confused mind will never buy, so make it easy for your prospects to choose you.

- So what do you want your brand to be known for? Trusted as the best at? Liked and wanted for?

Time to begin on the path to package together all your skills, talents, processes and systems, the transformation you deliver, and the passion and purpose behind your brand so you can set a course to be the leader and avoid wandering around in the bush or sailing about at the whim of the weather, going in all directions over the ocean.

Time to find your Brand True North, so you can make marketing and promoting your business a walk in the park.

"I can't change the direction of the wind,
but I can adjust my sails to always reach my destination."

~ Jimmy Dean

Finding Your Brand True North

A GOOD SAILOR understands they have to work with the conditions, know where they are headed, plot a course, and set their sails, regardless of what direction the wind is coming from. There are many things in life that you have little or no control over, but you do have control over your own destiny and your own brand.

Now that you are becoming clearer on what you want your brand to be known for, how you want to be recognised, what you want to be respected as the best for, and how you want people to refer to you, it's time to choose your brand direction, for your own personal brand and your business brand.

This is a question I get asked all the time: "What is the difference and do you need both?"

In reality our brains are constantly working to make sense of the world around us and brands help us do that. Regardless of whether we are defining a person or a business, a service or a product, our brains pigeonhole everything. This is why, if it takes too long for us to explain who we are, what we do, or why someone should choose us or our business, we can lose people's attention and get overlooked.

Consumers have very little time to absorb and process all the messages they see and even if they have a desire for your services, you will not even make it into their sphere of consciousness if you are not distinct.

As a leader, your personal brand flows over into the business brand. You help create the brand culture, the way people feel about dealing with you, trusting you or buying from you.

Today the consumer is in control. They no longer wait for you to present your services. If they have a problem they go looking for a solution. The first thing they do is Google it. They will search for and find any number of providers and then select who they feel they can trust. You can't control when they search for you, but you can control what they find.

Chances are there is a lot of content on your website and in your social media feed that is all about services, benefits, solutions, features. Very rarely do we share our passion, values, or core beliefs. Those are usually buried deep in the About page or hidden away at the bottom of the website, or not mentioned at all.

Your ideal prospect is looking for someone who has spent some time in their shoes, someone who cares about them and shares the same values.

Your ideal client is not searching for solutions; they don't know what the solution is. They are searching using words and terms based on their problem. By knowing where your brand is coming from and where it takes people, you can show them that not only do you understand their problem, you also have a solution for that problem and you have a real reason to care about solving it for them.

Your brand can give them an insight into who you are and what makes you passionate about what you do. They will start to feel they really know you and will connect more deeply with you, your brand, and your business.

Be careful not to be too flippant with your values or make things up that you think sound good. Pretending with no purpose, direction, or alignment between your personal values and the promise the business brand delivers will create a mis-match.

As the leader, it's up to you to keep on driving the brand message through everything the business does, or in the corporate world, what your team does and how it delivers.

If you don't align your personal brand with the business brand it is exhausting trying to make it happen rather than guiding it to happen.

I'm working long hours as production assistant in the direct marketing department at Saatchi & Saatchi[16]. I'm loving the vibe, even though the work is stressful and there are always deadlines looming. The creative teams are cool but crazy, the client service teams are demanding but driven. The agency has been rated in the top 10 in the world and there is a culture of excellence. People who work here know that they are world leaders.

There is a small rectangular room in the centre of the main floor, right next to the creative space. It's the creative lounge, a place where people can go to simply chill out, relax, and reflect. At the centre of the room is a beautiful paua[17] shell-infused resin-topped table, surrounded by lounge chairs. Covering every space of each wall are trophies, awards, and certificates. There are so many that there are bins on the floor full-to-brimming with awards and spikes on the wall with certificates impaled on them.

It is in this room that I find the art director I need to talk to about a project underway. As I walk into the lounge I meet the new copywriter being introduced to the team. This is how it works here, the creatives are matched in teams of two, one directing the creative imagery the other developing the copy. These are matches made in heaven—if they fit together they create the sort of advertising and brands that win awards.

It doesn't take long for everyone to know that the new guy doesn't fit. There is nothing wrong with him, he's a great guy, talented and creative. But something just doesn't feel right, for him or for others. No one is mean to him, everyone is welcoming and for a few days everyone gets on with it, but even he knows it's not working out. He leaves within a week. His personal brand didn't fit with the agency brand. Something was off.

---

[16] Saatchi & Saatchi is a British multinational communications and advertising agency network with 114 offices in 76 countries and over 6,500 staff. It was founded in 1970 and is currently headquartered in London. — https://en.wikipedia.org/wiki/Saatchi_&_Saatchi

[17] (Animals) an edible abalone, Haliotis iris, of New Zealand, having an iridescent shell used esp for jewellery [from Māori] — https://www.thefreedictionary.com/paua

It is the same with an awesome account manager I had worked with at a previous agency. She said she could never work at Saatchi's and she went to Clemenger[18] instead and loved it. I worked at both and enjoyed every minute of both, but there was a distinct difference in culture.

Not better or worse, just different.

Brand culture comes from the top down. As the leader for your business or being a leader within a corporate team, it is up to you to develop and cultivate the brand culture. People look to leaders to lead the way, not just in direction but also in manner and behaviour.

If your personal Brand True North is aligned with the business Brand True North this will come naturally to you and the brand culture will be incredibly easy to foster, nurture, and grow. The best part about this is that you are unique, your personal brand is like no other, so if you lead with your own brand, your business brand will also be unique.

Your DNA is unique. You have unique fingerprints, dental prints, and recent research has identified highly specific biochemical profiles in exhaled breath[x] that are unique to each person—yes, you even have a breath print!

So now that we know you are unique, what do you want to do with your life? What do you want your Brand True North to be all about?

---

[18] Clemenger Group Limited is the holding company of a group of companies involved in advertising and marketing communications throughout Australia and New Zealand. We operate across the marketing services spectrum with specialist companies offering clients best-of-category expertise in various disciplines. —https://www.clemenger.com.au/about

"The most difficult thing in life is to know yourself."

~ Thales

Who Do You Think You Are?

I DON'T KNOW how many times I've been asked this question by the adults in my life: "What do you want to be when you grow up?"

I have no idea! I love drawing, painting, being creative. But what sort of job is there that could I do with those skills? I like dancing, swimming, running, having adventures, being in nature. Is there a career in that? I grew up at a YMCA camp, meeting hundreds of new people all the time, and I'm confident to communicate with anyone. That's a useful skill to have right? My family come from the U.K. and I have heard tales of English history, seen photos of castles and tiny towns with thatched roofs. I'd love to travel. Maybe I should be an air hostess?

I tell people that and it seems to make them happy enough to leave me alone. Until one day my mother overhears me saying it and she takes me aside and tells me the chances of qualifying as an air hostess are not good as I have asthma and I'm probably too short. I toss away the idea of 'flying the friendly skies[19]' and try not to think too hard on what must be one of the most difficult questions children get asked.

As I finish high school I am still unsure what I want to be. I take a job in a bank and make money. It is the most sensible thing to do. My parents seem pleased.

Did you get asked this question as a child: "What will you be when you grow up?" How did it make you feel? Did you know for certain at a young age, what you were born to be and do? Not many do. Chances are you may still be asking yourself the question right now.

---

[19] Our iconic "Fly the Friendly Skies" tagline was reinvented in 2013 to reflect what's most important to our customers, as well as all that the word "friendly" encompasses in today's technology-driven world. — https://www.united.com/ual/en/us/fly/company/brand/advertising.html

As it turns out I want to be creative and while working at the bank I apply for and get into graphic design college. After qualifying, my first job in the industry is working for a service-based supplier to advertising agencies. Even though they don't mention it in the job interview, the training for my job sends me to London. I get to travel!

After a few years in the creative industry in New Zealand, I decide to travel again. I sell everything and live and work in Europe for five years. I have a range of jobs, some in advertising and printing, others behind the bar at the local pub, and even in a rock-climbing school. I sell newspaper ads, pubs, and timeshare. I have a blast learning sales and meeting people. On the weekends and holidays I enjoy visiting the castles and historic places I learnt about as a child.

When I return to New Zealand I get a job in publishing, then with a boutique ad agency, and eventually I work my way into world-leading agencies such as Saatchi & Saatchi, Clemenger BBDO, and Grey Worldwide[20]. I become a respected production manager, specialising in direct marketing and work for a large international corporate as Brand Manager, leading a team and I leverage a sponsorship deal to build brand awareness on a national scale. I start my own boutique agency, then move to Australia and launch into personal branding.

As it turns out, today I use *all* of the skills for what I thought might be possible jobs to do when I was a child, I get to do it all—be creative, travel, communicate, have adventures, rock climb, mountain bike, walk trails, and explore the world, while working in places I love.

Finding your Brand Truo North is all about taking a step backward from what you think you should *do* as a leader and look at what you want to *be* as a leader.

When you start a business as an entrepreneur, there is immense pressure to make money, to be profitable, to pay the

---

[20] Grey ranks among the world's top advertising and marketing agencies providing creative, experiential, social, digital, commerce and health & wellness expertise to one-fifth of the FORTUNE 500. —https://www.grey.com/en

mortgage. Your family are counting on you. As a leader in the corporate world, your success and the success of your team depends on how well you lead them. You are constantly under the scrutiny of your managers and your performance depends on the performance of your team. But making money for what you do is only one part of being a successful, stand-out leader.

When you start considering everything that makes you, you—your dreams, desires, plans, skills, talents, expertise and experience—suddenly it becomes more than just finding a way to earn a buck. It's about being fulfilled with a sense of purpose and pride that what you do is worth it.

Your brand makes you stand out because of your value, and that dictates how much you are paid.

Every single time I meet a leader and they tell me what they do for a living, I ask them the question, "What do you do and what makes you so different?" Most respond by talking about themselves or what makes them different from their competitors. Many try to explain the process they use or system they follow. Hardly anyone answers with how they transform people's lives, how they uniquely help deliver an outcome or how they make people feel.

But that's what real leaders primarily do and that's why people follow them—to feel good, to feel safe, or energised or happy or motivated.

We are going to discover your unique point of difference. This is the essence of your Brand True North. It encapsulates your purpose, making it easy to use the right marketing messages to become recognised and respected for what you do, with a reputation as the best leader for the job.

The first step with any brand development or rebranding is to review where your brand is at right now. Then you can decide if you are starting from the right spot and you can identify your core skills, key area of expertise, who you want to work with, and what sort of work and clients will be a total joy. Only then can you decide where you want to go and where you need to position your brand.

Your brand will help you create a legacy that extends well beyond profit, money, or paycheque.

Your brand will bring you fulfilment, happiness, and pride. It will give your marketing meaning, enabling you to have more impact and influence. But most of all, it will set you apart from your competition and give people a reason to follow your lead.

In an overwhelming and noisy world, it is increasingly difficult to be new, unique, or different. That's why we will follow a specific process to build your brand compass.

Many brands provide the same or similar services or products, but there is a reason why some are market leaders and others are also-rans. Most fall into the trap of trying to explain what makes them different by marketing quality, service, and delivery. These are all expected and not the exception. And you really don't want to differentiate on price, that's the 'race to the bottom'.

So what can you use to create a brand that stands out from the rest? How can you be unique when there are already so many others like you in the marketplace?

You already know that being consistent so you are instantly recognised and respected with a reputation as the go-to leader is the foundation of brand building. Now you need to define your USP, or 'Unique Selling Point.'

Remember that as a business owner your personal brand will flow over into your business brand. As a leader your drive, passion, and purpose will be what motivates and leads your team. Much in the same way Richard Branson's passion for helping others is distinctly sown into the Virgin brand, or Oprah Winfrey's focus on intention and purpose became HARPO's operating system, your personal brand will set a course for your brand values.

Knowing this, you can use the chapters that follow to pull together your very reason for being a leader, what makes you unique, special, or different, how you transform the lives of those who buy your products or services, and why they should care. It will also help your brand naturally attract the right opportunities, business partners, associates, team members, staff, affiliates, or franchisees, and the right clients.

In the following chapters we will go through each of the points of the compass helping you find your way to define and build your brand.

We will delve deeper into your brand purpose, target avatar, core message, and even some neurobranding science to help you not only package your brand, but also create a brand identity and implement marketing strategies *that work*.

Just like being lost in the bush or lost at sea, the following exercise will help you get clear on your direction, gathering together all the strands of your business expertise and power as an entrepreneur, business owner, leader, and fulfilled human being so you can find your way to the top.

The learning curve is going to be steep. You may find it exhausting at times. But when you get to the summit, the view will be breathtaking! And more importantly, you will clearly be able to see where you are going and how to get there.

So let's get started.

"If you're walking down the right path and you're willing to keep walking, eventually you'll make progress."

~ Barack Obama

YOUR BRAND COMPASS

THE FIRST STEP in finding your True North is to create your brand compass to keep you aligned and on purpose. This book will guide you to navigate through the four points of the compass.

Each point of the compass will help you define and package your brand. You can go through this process for your personal brand and for your business brand. If you work under a franchise brand or corporate brand, you can use this compass to ensure the content you create and your marketing message is aligned with the business brand.

You can also use this exercise to help your teams understand why your brand and business do things a certain way. When you give purpose to your actions, it is easier for everyone to align and get on the same path, working together for a common goal.

Here is the brand compass that we will cover in the following chapters:

WEST

What the problem is that you solve, for whom, why they have it, and what makes your brand the one they want.

EAST

Your expertise, how you execute what you do differently than everyone else, and how you explain it.

SOUTH

The value your brand delivers, the way you transform people, and the outcome that makes your brand so worthwhile.

NORTH

The passion and purpose that keeps you on True North. Your legacy and impact you want to have on the world.

YOUR BRAND COMPASS creates the foundations of your personal brand purpose, objective, values, and vision, so you can get 100 percent clear on what your brand stands for and what makes your brand different and unique. Then you can create your MAP, a *marketing action plan* to implement your brand message.

The good news is, from right now, you are no longer lost. You are about to use one of the most powerful tools to find your way to becoming the stand-out leader you know you are.

We are going to get started at West.

WEST

"The happiest and most successful people I know don't just love what they do, they're obsessed with solving an important problem, something that matters to them."

~ Drew Houston, Dropbox Co-Founder

THE PROBLEM

DRAGGING MY BAG through the crowded airport trying to avoid scampering children and ladies with unruly trolleys, businessmen juggle takeout coffee with briefcases. I eventually stumble into the final barrier to reaching my gate, the duty-free shopping area.

Duty-free is bursting with bright-coloured boxes and shiny perfume bottles. A favourite treat catches my eye—bright yellow, triangular, and tempting—a Toblerone[21] Bar. I know at once this is the ideal gift to take to my destination. After all, who doesn't love Swiss chocolate?

You probably know exactly what a Toblerone bar looks like, but do you know the story behind the brand? Do you know why it has a place in our brains as special, pure, Swiss chocolate, even though it's not actually made there?

In the early 1900s Emil Baumann and Theodor Tobler create a recipe for chocolate[xi] that also includes white nougat, almonds, and honey. Theodor, inspired by the shape of the mountainous land surrounding Berne where he was born, develops the distinctive triangular shape for the chocolate bar and the packaging. The name 'Toblerone' is a blend of words which translated literally mean, "Tobler's Nougat." The logo for the chocolate is of the Matterhorn[22] and inside the mountain is the shape of an animal, the icon of the city of Berne, a bear.

---

[21] Toblerone Swiss Milk Chocolate Candy Bar features iconic packaging and a distinctive taste that's been loved for over 100 years. Featuring Swiss milk chocolate filled with almond and honey nougat, Toblerone chocolate bars are crafted with high-quality ingredients to satisfy the tastes of any chocolate lover. —https://www.target.com/p/toblerone-swiss-milk-chocolate-candy-bar-12-6oz/-/A-12954413

[22] The Matterhorn is the Mountain of Mountains. Shaped like a jagged tooth, it's a magnet for adventurers looking for a mythical climb in Switzerland. — https://www.zermatt.ch/en/matterhorn

Now, you wouldn't think chocolate solves any problems, but of course it does. When we eat chocolate endorphins are released into our system making us feel all warm and fuzzy. Chocolate makes us happy and many turn to it to feel better or to find comfort. What better to nosh on if you feel you are in the cold snowy mountains of Switzerland than some nice triangular-shaped chocolate? You'd feel as cosy as a hibernating bear.

It's a comfort story told simply and very cleverly hidden in the brand of a chocolate that is now wholly owned by a company in Chicago, USA.

Toblerone seeks to solve a bigger problem too. It's the perfect last-minute gift idea as you battle your way home from a holiday or business trip and remember while you are about to board your flight that you have someone meeting you at home. Who would be unhappy about receiving a bar of Toblerone as a gift? Everyone loves that triangular box of yumminess!

Who would have thought that chocolate solves a problem?

Toblerone demands a premium that other chocolate brands can't attract.

But be careful of changing your brand promise. When the manufacturers tried to reduce the amount of chocolate in each bar by spreading out the triangular sections consumers knew about it and complained.

What your brand stands for and the problem it solves is your WEST. WEST stands for WHAT, WHO, WHEN and WHY:

- What is the problem your brand solves?
- Who has it most?
- When do they have it?
- What makes the problem turn into a pain?
- Why do they have the pain?
- What has lead them to this point where they need you?
- Why would they choose your brand?

So often in marketing we fail to identity the problem we solve and go straight to promoting our services and solutions, however the secret to having a sought-after brand is to find the problem first.

Knowing your ideal prospect and the problem they have is key, and I suggest developing a *target avatar* to achieve this. A target avatar is a profile of your ideal client, constructed from as much information you can about their life so that you can better understand their needs and what sort of brand message and marketing will best attract and connect with them.

WEST is all about defining your ideal client—your target avatar—and discovering how your brand solves their problem.

Target avatars can be complicated, with many developing multiple avatars or using themselves as the avatar. So let's make it easy. Defining your target avatar is like climbing a Swiss mountain. Key Opinion Leaders (KOLs) are at the top of the mountain. They are influencers and people listen to them. Their opinions matter and you can create an avalanche of influence, leveraging their influence if you get your brand in front of them.

Looking up to them are your ideal clients (those worth climbing for). They listen to the KOLs and they want to overcome their problems. They are looking for a leader to help them get to the summit of success.

Everyone below them are like trolls. They are in the dark and don't think they have a problem to solve. They probably don't even realise there is a mountain to climb. They need convincing to even take one step. They complain and fight back and are hard to work with. They are not worth focusing on.

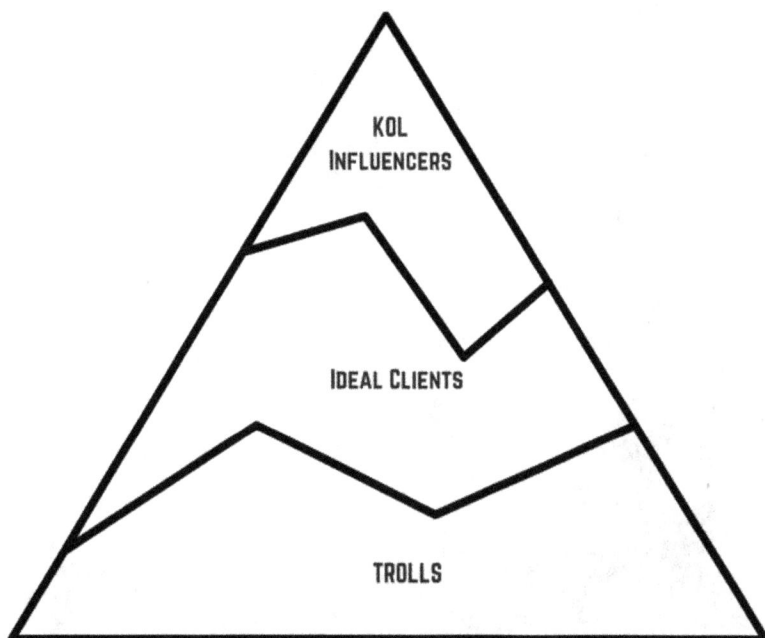

If you don't know what mountain you are climbing, or you are targeting people who don't want or need your brand, you will wear yourself out, chasing prospects all over the countryside.

Worse, if you try to climb too many mountains at the same time, it's exhausting and puts your business at risk of failure or devaluing your brand by being unfocused and desperate.

Great brands focus on the ideal audience and put all their effort into attracting the right people. They know exactly who they want to engage with and they don't waste time, effort, or money going after everyone.

I'm clearing out the post box outside the apartment building where we live. As I lean down to open the box with my key, the sun reflects off the metal, temporarily blinding me. The junk mail pours out of the box and onto the pavement. *Damn it.*

I catch the last of the mail falling from the box and bend down to collect the rest. Poking out from the white envelopes is a blue business card. I stop what I am doing to read what's on the card. As I read the words I begin to smile, then grin. I throw my head back and laugh. I know this card will be the perfect example of how not to position your brand. I take my phone out from my pocket and take a photo of it before taking the card and the rest of my mail inside.

CHEAP MAN AND UTE HIRE
MINI MOVES BIG MOVES ANYTHING

FURNITURE PICK UP

HOUSE MAINTENANCE / LIFTS TO SHOPPING CENTRES, DOCTORS ECT
HELP LIFTING FURNITURE/ HELP SHIFTING
PET FEEDING / WALKING / ANIMAL TRANSPORT

LAWN MOWING GARDEN MAINTENANCE RUBBISH REMOVAL
ELVIS TRIBUTE LIVE MUSIC 50'S 60'S 70'S ROCK N ROLL
JUMPING CASTLE HIRE LIMOUSINE HIRE
0431 755 005   OPEN 24 HRS 7 DAYS ALL HOLIDAYS

Do you think this is a well-trusted, stand-out brand? Would you recommend this brand? At least he is 'on-brand' in terms of his promise—cheap. But, what if he had just chosen two of those deliverables, like mowing lawns dressed as Elvis? I would pay to see that and I don't even own a house with a lawn.

If he chose a niche and targeted the right audience, he would be well-known, in the media, referred to, and recommended. He could scale his business, adding more Elvis's or branching out into other services. He could expand his business, with Marilyn Monroe cleaning your house or James Dean fixing your car.

But no, he is trying to do too much, wearing too many hats and trying to be everything to everyone. He is trying to climb too many mountains. He has failed to learn the first lesson of branding: *Having a clear WEST.*

You can't help every Mary in the dairy.

Consider how much of your time is spent doing things you shouldn't be doing. Are you chasing after the wrong sort of client, offering too many options, and climbing too many mountains? How much time and money are you wasting on marketing activity that doesn't get results or social media and promotion that are not helping you reach your goals? Is your brand message having the right impact on the right people? Is it clear who you help and the problem you solve for them?

It's time to get 100 percent clear on what problem you want your brand to solve and start focusing on the summit of your mountain, the one you most want to reach in order to become known by the key opinion leaders (KOLs) who will refer business to you.

If you want to avoid WOFTAM and be seen and known as the #1 leader in your category, choose one mountain to climb.

Let's define your ideal target avatar. Let's start climbing *that* mountain.

YOUR MOUNTAIN

I'M WANDERING THROUGH the blocked-off main street of the Sunday markets in the suburbs near our home in Queensland, Australia. It's still early and not too hot or busy yet. I have my list and I'm taking my time wandering amongst the blue and white sunshades, chatting to the stall holders.

I find the forest-honey man to refill my container and the farm-egg lady to get a fresh dozen. Before long my bag is full of fruit and vegetables and I can smell the sugary sweet Dutch pancakes that have started to cook at the stall on the corner.

While I wait for my pancake order, I check out the locally-made gifts, looking through the cotton clothing and marvelling at the colourful handmade bracelets. Then I spot a stand that intrigues me and I make my way over to find out more.

On the table there are white tubes of some sort of potion that I assume is hand cream. I have had eczema since I was a child and my hands and lips are always dry, so it's something I look out for. But I'm wrong, this isn't hand cream. Turns out the stall holder is an inventor and the tubes contain a special gel that he has created to give your hands grip. He tells me he plays sports and knows what it's like to lose grip on your tennis racket or golf club in the hot, humid weather we experience here in Queensland.

I'm intrigued and ask him how it's going and who is buying his products. He tells me he is trying to get it into the sports clubs, but has also had tradesmen buy it because it helps them keep a grip on their hammers and tools in the baking hot sun on worksites. But, he proudly tells me, his best clients are those he had no idea even existed. He leans in and, with a sparkle in his eyes and broad grin on his face he whispers two words: "pole dancers."

Turns out they need grip the most. It helps them stick to the pole during their acrobatics, giving them an edge over their competitors and helping them stay up in the air longer.

When it comes to defining your ideal client, it is vital that you know *who* is most likely to both need and want your services or products, *why* they need and want them, and *when* they are most likely to come looking for your mountain to climb. Only then can you start to understand *what* message to use and *when* is the best time and channel to use to captivate and appeal to them.

You want to target those climbing your mountain because they already have the pain or problem you solve. They are aware of it and are probably already looking for help, they just haven't seen your brand of solution yet.

Here are the three steps to identify the ideal target avatar who is climbing your mountain:

Step One: DEMOGRAPHICS

As long as you remember you are only creating one target avatar, that of the person who most wants and needs your services or products right now, defining your target avatar's demographics is pretty easy.

Don't worry that you might have a broad range of age, gender, or location for your potential buyers and followers. Demographics is just one element of the target avatar. Remember, we are defining exactly who is already climbing your mountain, those who already know they have the problem your brand solves.

Consider the demographics of your ideal prospect. What is the average age of the *best* client you could wish for? Are they settled with a partner, mortgage, kids and family, or pets? Or are they semi-retired, empty nesters, with grandchildren on the way, keen to travel and enjoy life as a priority?

Once you consider where your ideal audience is in their life stage, you can get really clear about where they live, what they do for work or income, how educated they are, what media they watch, read, or listen to, where they spend their hobby time, where they go on holiday, and so on. You can understand what makes them want to climb your mountain. What has happened in their life to make them seek out a leading brand to help them?

The thing about demographics is you can never learn too much. Just keep adding info to the list. Use Google and www.answerthepublic.com to find out what your ideal clients are searching for. Consider your best clients and think about their life stage. *You want more people like them!*

When you know what your ideal client is doing during the day, week, month, year, it's easy to figure out when to target them and with what message to be both relevant and timely.

Step Two: PSYCHOGRAPHICS[23]

Target marketing experts often talk about getting the right demographics: age, sex, marital status, geographical location, employment, religion, life stage, lifestyle. But it's vital you know more about your ideal customers than just where they live and what they do for a living. As mentioned before, age, gender, and location are only one aspect of your ideal client.

Psychographics gives you a deeper understanding of your target avatar. What drivers, beliefs, cultural mores (habits or customs), values they have. Psychographics enable you to step into their shoes and understand the reason why they want your brand, allowing you to have a broader demographic range of age, gender, and location. Values and beliefs are often developed in our formative years and influenced by family upbringing, peers, and the society we grow up in.

So think again of your ideal client. What sort of culture or society were they born into and grew up in? What were the

---

[23] Psychographics is the study of consumers based on their activities, interests, and opinions (AIOs). It goes beyond classifying people based on general demographic data, such as age, gender, or race. Psychographics seeks to understand the cognitive factors that drive consumer behaviors. This includes emotional responses and motivations; moral, ethical, and political values; and inherent attitudes, biases, and prejudices. — https://www.cbinsights.com/research/what-is-psychographics/

beliefs, habits, customs, and values they experienced? This way you can understand not only who and where they are, but also what drives them, how they think and feel about the problem you are solving for them, and who and what influences their decision-making. By understanding the emotional and value-driven feelings your ideal audience has, you can put yourself in their shoes and walk a while through the problem they have, gaining a better insight into why they might want what you have.

Psychographics are based on core beliefs, values, mores and generational traits that help people form their opinions. For example:

- Someone born in 1940 values respect, considers that it is all about the team, not the individual, and doesn't want to be a burden on others.

- Someone born in the 60s might be more open to radical ideas, individuality, and rights, but respects systems and levels of class, and believes you work hard to get ahead.

- A 1980s baby will have different ideas about affluence, independence, and borrowing money to someone born in the 60s.

- Someone born in the early 2000s is all about personal development and individuality, focuses on the now and what they are owed.

It's not better or worse, it's just that our beliefs and values are formed by the world around us.

Consider cultural values as well. Family is treated very differently in some cultures compared to others. For example, you wouldn't dream of putting aged parents into a rest home in Asia, the expectation is that children take care of their parents at home.

The main consideration with psychographics is to determine what *feelings* and *emotions* your target avatar has that are driving their search for your solution and what will make them choose your brand. What opinions are they likely to have about how your brand solves their problem? This helps you understand not just when the pain occurs but also how they feel about it.

A good exercise is to record a day in the life of your ideal prospect from when they wake to when they go to bed:

- What are they focused on?
- What do they do and say to others and to themselves?
- How do they feel?
- And when do they consider needing help?

Record it as a conversation. It should take no more than 15 minutes. Then get it transcribed and turned into a Word (Pages, or other word processing) document. There are a load of transcription services out there, just Google them. My favourites are REV.com and speechpad.com or otter.ai.

Once you have your day in the life in a document, grab a highlighter pen and start noting the specific words and phrases that could become marketing headlines, blog topics, video content, and so on. If you can use the words your target avatar is saying to themselves in your marketing, they will instantly connect and engage with your brand message.

You will discover the value of this exercise when you are developing your marketing action plan later in this book.

Step Three: PERSONAL COMMUNICATION STYLE (PCS)

Combining demographics with psychographics helps you understand where your target audience is on the mountain, why they are climbing it, and how they feel about being there. Now it's time to discover how to communicate with them, so they choose you as their guide to the summit of success.

Knowing what is going on in their life and how they feel about it will help you understand what has led them to this point, why they are seeking your services or products and what has motivated them to look for help.

Now you can add the final factor that can make marketing incredibly effortless and instinctive for you and your brand and kick off that avalanche of influence, increasing the opportunity for all of your ideal prospects to engage with your brand.

Communication

Great brands communicate so well with you (their clients) in the way they know you will engage, connect, and buy, that you don't even know they are doing it. You will uncover examples of this as you journey through this book.

Research has shown that humans are hopeless at picking up on signals from each other, misreading the situation more than 50 percent of the time[xii] so it's vital that when your brand is in front of your prospect, you don't screw up how you deal with them. Knowing how your ideal customer or client likes to be communicated with is simple once you know the *four Personal Communication Styles*. This technique is used by most good salespeople and it doesn't come naturally to everyone, but you can learn it. If you understand and apply it to your brand message, you can become the #1 chosen brand people love.

By tapping into how humans naturally communicate, the emotional and mental needs for security and the emotional drivers behind why we buy, you can create the right brand message with ease. The first step is to understand your natural style of communicating. Once you know your own, you can easily recognise it in others. Once you understand *Personal Communication Styles* (PCS) you can make sure that the images, language, and messages you use to promote your brand will instantly engage your prospects, inspiring them to take action and choose you.

Imagine you are at a car sales yard. A good salesperson will quickly discover how you like to be communicated with, what information you want, and how you like that information to be presented. That way all of the questions you might ask the salesperson are answered in a way you feel comfortable with, making you more agreeable and more likely to trust. By using the communication style you are most comfortable with the salesperson has made you feel like they know you and have your best interests at heart.

But how does this relate to branding and marketing?

Personal communication style (PCS) is basically how we are all individually wired to respond to marketing and promotional material. Your Personal Communication Style relates to the preferred way you like to communicate and be communicated with. We use all four Personal Communication Styles at different times, but one will be the dominant and the most comfortable way you like to be communicated with when you are seeking information in order to make a purchase decision.

To make it simple for you, I have used birds to code the different styles. Each bird has a different communication style. Let's take a closer look at all four Personal Communication Styles:

Eagles

Eagles are born leaders, driven by results, outcomes and deliverables. The *end result* is their total goal and objective. They don't need to know all the details of how they will get there, they just need to trust you will help them achieve it. They can come across as abrupt or uncaring because their communication style is fast, succinct, and focused. Don't waste time on pleasantries with Eagles.

When it comes to working with others, their abrupt communication style scares the hell out of the Doves; the Peacocks think they are rude; and the Owls don't trust them at all! They like punchy headlines, fewer words, lots of pictures and anything that clearly shows them the outcome. Quick videos, animations or explainer style infographics are awesome for Eagles. Whatever you do, don't make them take too many steps to get to the sale. Once they want something, they will buy, but be aware, they will change to another provider if it looks like a better deal.

Peacocks

Peacocks are social creatures. They love connecting, networking, and talking. They will be the first to gather at the office water cooler on a Monday morning. Engagement and real connection are vital to them in order to communicate. They like meeting in person and love being part of a team. Having fun while doing something is a core desire. The journey is as important as the outcome.

They dislike boring tedious or repetitive communication and will annoy the Eagles who just want them to get to the point. They worry the Doves because they think Peacocks always say something silly and embarrassing and the Owls detest the Peacocks drama and wonder how they ever get anything done.

Peacocks like stories and love to show off their purchases or share their wins. The more background you can give them the better. They really enjoy experiential marketing they can immerse themselves in and will get into interactive media as long as it's fun. They are great at recommending brands to others. Your ideal Key Opinion Leaders are often Peacocks because they create a following. They're also the first to complain and write bad reviews so take time to listen to them.

Owls

Owls are facts and figures communicators. They like to know all the options and they do their research and take time to evaluate everything before making a decision. Owls will encourage others to think of all the options and outcomes and love it when their ideas are proven to be the best. They are highly competitive and will go out of their way to strategize how they can come out on top.

Owls think Eagles are rash and reckless, Peacocks are frustrating time wasters, and they know they can rely on the Doves to communicate clearly without fuss.

Giving Owls time to absorb all the information before they buy is vital. They will want all the spec sheets, brochures, product details, contracts, data and information, and they will want to compare it all before they choose to trust you as their leader. Don't rush them and make sure you give them everything they need. If you win over an Owl, they will provide lots of referrals.

Doves

Doves are team players. They like things to go smoothly and prefer communications that lay out the system or process. They are caring, thoughtful, and always consider what's best for everyone. They remember details that are meaningful and tend to work behind the scenes, making sure everyone is happy. Never put a Dove in the spotlight, make too much of a fuss of them, or spring change on them, expecting them to adapt and deal with it. They like responsibility and finishing tasks. Keeping everything going is enough to know they are valuable.

Doves are interested in the big picture. What will the service or product deliver to the entire household or workplace? They want to know about guarantees, delivery, and quality. They want to try before they buy, love samples, and will be very loyal if looked after well.

You can take a quiz here to find out what your dominant PCS is:
www.yourbrandtruenorth.com/pcsquiz

We use all four Personal Communication Styles at different times and the one we use most will depend on what we are doing. For example:

1. If you have a contract to read your Owl style will be dominant;

2. A sick child to look after and you will use Dove style communication traits;

3. At a party and breaking the ice, your Peacock style will come to the fore;

4. Being asked to lead a presentation, you will call on your Eagle Personal Communication Style to help you get it done.

However, we will have one style that is most dominant for most of the time. It is the way we prefer to be communicated with. For example most people like coffee but the brand they choose will come down to how they connect with the brand message. At times however you may not get a choice and it's a decision made by convenience or location.

Applying PCS to branding and marketing is easy. Here is a test for you to spot which brand message appeals most to each of the four Personal Communication Styles:

- Of course, the Eagles with their no-nonsense requirement connect instantly with the Nike value of Just Do It;
- Peacocks love the social elements of the Coke brand message;
- Owls respect the way BMW communicates all the data and information;
- Doves align with equality focused Benetton.

All of us will at one time or another engage with or buy all four of these brands. But we will have favourites, choosing by the way the brand conducts itself or selecting a brand that is naturally more appealing or communicates with us in a way we naturally feel comfortable.

Now you have a better idea of who is climbing your mountain. Remember:

- Demographics are only one element telling you why they are there,
- Psychographics will help you know how they feel about it,
- PCS will help you communicate better with them in your marketing.

Now you have the three-step process you can use to make sure you are focusing on the right people:

1. **DEMO**: Understand who your target audience is by gathering the geographic and demographic information, their life stage and lifestyle, knowing why they are climbing your mountain.

2. **PSYCHO**: Investigate the psychographics by considering their feelings and emotions, putting yourself in their shoes, or taking a look at the world they grew up in that shaped their values and beliefs that make them feel a certain way about being on your mountain.

3. **PCS**: The natural communication style to work out what information they need and how they prefer to be communicated with in order to get to the summit of success, with you as their leader.

You can now give them exactly what they want and need in the right way, so they can keep coming up that mountain to know, like, and trust you as the leading brand. You can now position yourself as a Key Opinion Leader at the top of your mountain so more of your ideal clients can follow you.

But there is one last thing you need to understand about your target avatar, especially if you want to earn trust as a new leader on the top: *human behaviour is much harder to change than attitude.*

We all know it's not healthy to smoke, yet tobacco companies still make millions selling their products. We know going to the dentist for an annual check-up is vital for our long-term ability to eat properly, but we put off or avoid going to the dentist.

You can change a human's attitude towards something, making sure they know the risks or dangers or enticing them to venture onto new pathways and to follow a new leader, but getting them to stray from a competitor's mountain to climb yours is harder than it sounds.

Here's a fun neurobranding exercise you can do to demonstrate exactly how powerful our brains are at keeping us safe, making sure we override new things with the things we know. Ready? Here it goes (I hope you are not in a public place while you are reading this book!):

- Just for a moment, point your leg out in front of you and start turning your foot in a clockwise direction.

- Awesome. Now lift your arm, point your index finger in the air in front of you, and draw the number six (6). Notice what happens to your foot? That's right, it starts turning the other way.

Your brain overrides something you hardly ever do (such as twirling your foot around in a clockwise motion) with something it has done for many years (writing the number six).

And it happened instantly.

This is why when you are marketing and promoting your brand to new prospects you can confuse and alienate the very people you are trying to help. They fear the unknown. And they don't know you yet. Your brand is a stranger to them. Their brain is screaming at them to stay safe and not make any risky decisions. So you are already on the back foot.

If you take the time to really get to know exactly who has the problem you solve, you can put that at the core of your target avatar. Knowing what is going on in their life and how they feel about it and then resonating, engaging, and communicating perfectly with them to sell your products or services as the solution will be a walk in the park.

The last thing you want to do when you are promoting your professional services to gain new customers is to start introducing even more 'new' to them. Just like when your brain overrides something new with what it knows (the foot and finger exercise you just did) if your brand is new or you are trying to get prospects to do something new, changing behaviour or introducing yourself as the new leader, you need to take time to become familiar and earn trust.

When exposed to a new idea or being asked to do something differently our brains switch into overdrive trying to figure out the situation. Prospects will not be listening to your marketing message if they are fearful. Their brains will be too busy trying to figure out who you are, what you can do to help them, and if you can do anything *for them*. If you overcomplicate your message your ideal customers' brains will shut down and run.

Avoid talking too soon about your solution, services, tech, apps, or processes in your marketing. Certainly don't start a sales pitch and never, ever start talking about what you want to achieve as a result of your promotion.

It's the first rule in sales, it's the same rule in marketing, and it's the same for creating a stand-out brand as a leader in business:

Know your customer.

Avalanche Of Influence

I PUT THE RECEIVER of the phone down and stare at the wall in disbelief. Shaking my head I get up from my chair and go upstairs to my business partner's office. I knock on the door and go in.

"What's up?" he says.

"Well, I just had the oddest of calls," I start explaining. "The owner of a hardware store in a country region just called to say he wasn't ever going to stock our product, in fact he is telling anyone who comes into his store to go down the road to his competitor to buy it and he requested that we stop promoting it because too many people are coming in asking for it!"

We stare at each other in disbelief for a few seconds then we both burst out laughing.

This is the power of creating an avalanche of influence.

Just six months earlier we took over the marketing of a brand-new gardening product, something the market had never seen before. It wasn't a bug spray or a fertiliser, it was a new science called *biomimicry*. As with most inventions not only is there a huge amount of education required to get people to try it, there is also next-to-no budget.

We found a list of all the garden clubs in the back of a magazine and paid someone to call them all to find out who in the club would be best to 'test' the product to see if it worked. Of course, we knew it would work, but we wanted to give them the chance to prove something to us. We also gave the club coupons for big discounts on the product for their members.

We then mailed packs out to around 500 of these Key Opinion Leaders who were members of gardening clubs, with a small sample bottle of the product, a personalised letter, a brochure about how to use it, and a tracker, plus a self-addressed return envelope for them to send us the photos of their test after six weeks.

Most direct marketing campaigns have a 2 percent response rate, but within a few months we had a whopping 43 percent of all packs sent back to us with testimonials and photos. We had avid gardeners from all over the country sending us letters, trackers, and images, raving about how big their cabbage was or how beautiful their roses were, how wonderful their flowers smelled or how the bugs didn't eat all their tomatoes.

At the same time we targeted the early adopters (the Key Opinion Leaders who had influence in their local communities and gardening clubs) we also targeted a select group of gardening journalists and editors, hoping to score a couple of well-known KOLs too. Fortunately, an award-winning garden photographer, a print journalist, and a radio host all loved the product and they started raving about it in the media. Within nine months we had garden shops around the country calling to ask if they could stock our products. We were in 75 stores within 18 months.

Now, let's put this in perspective.

Normally, brands have to pitch to retailers to have their product on the shelf and even then they have to prove the product will sell and be in demand. New products also have to provide lots of marketing support to the stores, sales collateral, and stands. Many pay for shelf space.

We not only had shops *asking us* if they could sell the product, they also invited us to go to the stores to do demonstrations, hold talks, and set up stands in the front of the stores. We had lots of shelf coverage right next to big-name brands who had probably paid a lot of money just to be there. We also had one very unusual store ask us to stop promoting because he had too many people coming in asking for it!

Creating an avalanche of influence does take time and effort but if you don't have the big budgets of Coca-Cola, McDonald's, or Nike, it's a really effective way to get your brand in front of people who will share, refer, and sell it to those below them who are climbing your mountain.

For a start you can become a Key Opinion Leader and influencer yourself. Find where your target avatar is hanging out and get invited to speak on the podcasts they listen to, write articles for the blogs or magazines they read. You are positioning yourself as a leader in that space and you can trigger an avalanche of influence by getting in front of your target audience as often as possible and having others share your content.

The best way to set off an avalanche of influence however, is when you know who your target avatar looks up to and identify the influencers at the top.

For example, with the telecommunications mountain, tech-geeks are at the summit of the 'phone mountain,' pulling apart the technology, reviewing the apps, giving their opinion on the best camera or speed or value. They are the ones who early adopters of technology follow. They provide the reviews, podcasts, blogs, or YouTube review videos that the ideal consumers of phones read, listen to, and watch.

If you are a phone brand like Apple or Samsung, you want the KOLs to favourably review your devices so they send an avalanche of influence down to the ideal prospective clients who are climbing your mountain. These are the people who camp outside the store when the latest device is launched. They want to be market leaders, but they don't have the influence of the KOLs and they have to buy their way in.

The early adopters are ideal prospective clients who are climbing the mountain, looking up to the KOLs for advice and making purchase decisions based on what the leaders at the top are saying and doing. This is why Apple, Samsung and many others get their devices into the hands of celebrities, influencers, and endorsers who will 'spruik' the product before it is available, creating demand and triggering that avalanche.

The last thing these brands want to do is waste time trying to convince the trolls, those who still have Nokia phones, or conspiracy theorists with non-smart phones, who will never want what Apple or Samsung offer.

It's a moonless night out on the wooden deck at the back of the small house in the middle of nowhere and it is getting cold. We are here to celebrate a birthday and the pizza oven has delivered dinner nicely, but is no longer providing sufficient heat for the guests who are gathered together with drinks in hand. Jackets are retrieved from the bedroom and woollen hats are pulled down over our ears so we can stay out and enjoy the clear night of stars above our heads.

The last of the light from the sunset is gone and the night sky is beginning to twinkle all around us. With no street lights nearby the Milky Way and all the constellations are bright and crisp. Many of the guests are pointing into the blackness with questioning discussions about which star is which. It is easy to identify the Southern Cross[24] and Orion[25] with his belt and sword but what about that bright star closer to the horizon that seems to be changing colour?

"It's not a star, it's Mars," says the familiar voice of my husband and everyone is impressed with his celestial know-how. They all want to know how he knows it is not a star, but a planet. He calmly turns to face the group and brings his arm out in front of him to expose to us all that he is no genius of the heavens, he is instead holding his phone up to the sky and is using an app to identify everything that comes into view.

Suddenly everyone pulls out their own phone and wants to know the app name so they can download it and share in the sky-scanning. Once downloaded, we are all pointing our phones heavenward and being amazed at the information we gather.

---

[24] Crux (/krʌks/) is a constellation of the southern sky that is centred on four bright stars in a cross-shaped asterism commonly known as the Southern Cross. It lies on the southern end of the Milky Way's visible band. The name Crux is Latin for cross. —https://en.wikipedia.org/wiki/Crux

[25] Orion is a prominent constellation located on the celestial equator and visible throughout the world. It is one of the most conspicuous[1] and recognizable constellations in the night sky.[2] It is named after Orion, a hunter in Greek mythology. —https://en.wikipedia.org/wiki/Orion_(constellation)

There is the constellation Scorpio, that's Venus up there, and over there is Sirius, the dog-star.

The man next to me lowers his phone beneath the horizon and exclaims in surprise to see that he can identify stars and planets beneath his feet! But how can that be?

I tell him he is looking at the constellations through the Earth and seeing what is in the Northern Hemisphere. He is amazed and awestruck, until I say, "Yes, it's amazing isn't it? And if you bend over far enough you'll see Uranus!"

The entire party on the deck cracks up laughing, the phones are put back into pockets, and the party gets underway again with engaging conversations, storytelling, and friendships continuing to be made.

Technology is awesome. It is clever and it mostly makes our lives easier. But it is also a distraction. For decades seafarers used the stars to navigate to their destination. The guiding lights are always there to quickly and efficiently help you get to where you want to go. The stars stay in place and all you need to do is know which one you want to aim for in order to make your brand and business shine.

If you really want your brand to stand out and be known as the #1 in your industry you need to reach out and connect with your community, making enough impact that you generate the momentum needed to be seen as the leader.

Now you know your target avatar you can target them based on their life stage, lifestyle, and also on their emotional need and desire for your solution. You can now create an impact on the Key Opinion Leaders they look up to, those at the top of your mountain, those who influence the decision-making of your ideal prospects or hold the key to the door of your success as a leader.

Our phones make it easy to search online and through social media for exactly who we need to get our brand in front of, but once you have found them don't get distracted by technology and bogged down in text messaging, DMing, or emailing.

The fastest way to get to your Key Opinion Leaders and start creating an avalanche of influence is to call them and talk to them. So often we are afraid to pick up the phone and do what it was intended for—make a call. Instead, we stalk people and hide behind our keyboards, posting, commenting, and sharing, hoping that the person we want to get in front of will see us and want to connect. So use your phone to find your stars, those prospective connections and influencers who will set off an avalanche of influence amongst your ideal prospects, and early adopters, but make sure you converse with them. Start up a relevant and helpful conversation and call them!

Make a list of the KOLs—those who impact your avatar—the leaders in the community they seek out for advice or those they follow online. Reach out to these influencers, follow them on social media, like, comment, share. Give them some love and associate yourself with their brands.

Look for symbiotic relationships. Like the clownfish and the sea anemone, where the fish gets shelter and the anemone gets cleaned and protected from other fish. Find those who have the same type of client but don't provide the service or product you do. Find a win-win opportunity, make affiliations and partnerships, consider how you can help them. A few examples:

- Landscape gardeners | pool cleaners | painters and decorators
- Mortgage brokers | real estate agents | property lawyers
- Bookkeepers | accountants | financial planners
- Swimming instructors | personal trainers | gym/Pilate/yoga studios
- Business coaches | insurance advisors | human resources specialists

Some of the most successful brand partnerships have been between stand-out brands that share audiences but don't complete. They teamed up to create more impact as leaders.

One of the earliest big brand collaborations and a no-brainer in my opinion—Nike and iPod created fitness trackers and sneakers along with clothing that tracked the customer's activity while connecting them to their favourite tunes. Beat that!

GoPro gives athletes and adventurers around the world tools and funding to capture things like races, stunts, and action sports events on video, all from the athlete's perspective. Red Bull uses its experience and reputation to run and sponsor the events these athletes appear in. Together they are a match made in heaven.

Both known for quality, two traditional brands that are all about high-quality craftsmanship, BMW created a sports car called the BMW i8 and Louis Vuitton designed an exclusive four-piece set of suitcases and bags that fit perfectly into the car's rear parcel shelf. Car-boom!

Two shopping brand giants, Amazon who wanted to improve the way small businesses sell on their platform, and American Express created a co-branded credit card, sharing the purchase activity data and adding credibility to each other's brands. Ka-ching!

When you look at your brand values to check your Brand True North you can find who else is operating in your space with the same audience but different services or products. You can align your activity and benefit from the joint marketing and promotion, tapping into each other's followings and making a far bigger impact.

Here are some points to consider:

- What brands are like yours but not competing for the same customer?
- Which brands have the same values as you?
- Who is creating a solution your customers want, that you don't cater to?
- Who is doing a great job of marketing, but is missing a piece of the puzzle that you could offer?
- What brands would you like to be seen with for some 'branding by association?'

- If you had an 'Intel inside," what would that be and who makes that?

To figure out who the ideal brands and KOLs are best to team up with it can be as easy as figuring out where in the food chain your service sits. Who provides something to your ideal client before they need you? Who provides something after you?

Mike O'Hagan, founder of Mini-Movers, once shared a very clever tactic that his removal company used to constantly fill their funnel with prospective ideal clients and it was also a brilliant way to build brand awareness at exactly the right time for his audience.

He asked me, "When do you most need a removal company?"

My response: "When you buy or sell a home."

By understanding where in the food chain their service was, the Mini-Movers team could gather information from the internet of all the houses for sale in the areas they serviced. It was easy to get the data and turn that into a sales opportunity simply by letting the prospective client know that when the time is right, Mini-Movers are there to help. It's an ideal way to kick off an avalanche of influence, getting in front of your prospects as they climb that mountain of need and letting them know you are there when they need you.

To set off the avalanche of influence on your mountain, all you have to do is get your brand known by a handful of KOLs at the top. Make contact with these service providers and leaders to let them know your brand exists so the next time they have your ideal client in front of them they can instantly refer them to you when the time is right. Here are the steps:

1. Creating a list of the KOLs you want to get to know.
2. Figure out what you can do to help each other.
3. Connect with them, call and arrange a meeting.
4. Partner on projects, run events together, create programs, or provide collaborated services.

Develop a system of referrals so you are jointly promoting each other's brands and helping each other's businesses.

Don't be afraid to talk to the KOLs. Remember, they are leaders just like you. They have the same challenges, stresses, fears and worries as leaders. They also have the same goals and desires to be respected and wanted. Find relevant and reasonable reasons to contact them and keep your brand front of mind by sending them useful information and leads. Consider how you can support each other as leaders. It can be lonely in business being the owner of a company, the head of a corporate organisation, or an entrepreneur.

If you put in the effort and create a big enough impact at the top of the mountain, you can set off an avalanche of influence where you are all receiving and giving referrals constantly to each other and your business. Brand awareness and personal brand credibility all grow when you work together.

Now that you know the WEST of your brand compass and what you need to do to get clear on what the problem is that your brand solves, it's time to move on to EAST.

EAST

"You have brains in your head. You have feet in your shoes.
You can steer yourself in any direction you choose.
You're on your own, and you know what you know.
And you are the guy who'll decide where to go."

~ Dr. Seuss

EXPERT-EASE

IN 1948 TWO brothers-in-law combine their businesses to become Baskin-Robbins. At the time, one brother's business has 21 flavours and the other has 10, so combining them means Baskin-Robbins now has 31 flavours. As the ice cream market becomes increasingly competitive with some offering chunkier or fruitier or creamier flavours, Baskin-Robbins stick with their brand position, the thing that makes them different, their Unique Selling Proposition (USP) of having at least 31 flavours available.

They deliver a unique brand promise that customers can try as many flavours as they like before deciding on which ones they want in their cone. The Baskin-Robbins brand promise, the #1 thing the brand does differently than everyone else in the market that makes them stand out from the competition, is represented with a logo that tells their brand story. The B and the R of the logo form the number 31:

Baskin-Robbins is one of the most prolific franchise brands in the world with over 8,000 stores globally. The brand is known, liked, and trusted. They still to this day deliver on their promises.

- So what is your type of ice cream?
- What makes you stand out from the rest?
- What do you and your brand do differently that others do not?
- What special skills or natural talents do you use that no one else can claim to have?
- Have you developed a unique approach or process?
- How has your brand innovated or specialised?
- What does your brand promise to deliver that no one else can do?

In order to stand out and be respected as the leading brand, you need to go further than the usual promises of quality or service. Everyone offers that. Good workmanship, professionalism, sustainability, and value are all things customers expect. They are not enough to make your brand stand out. They do not provide a level of expertise that delivers the special factor that leading brands possess, brands that attract devotion of loyal clients, command a premium, and attract opportunities others do not, brands that have a clear point of difference.

The DNA for this is embedded into the foundation of why the brand exists, and everyone knows it.

EAST stands for Expert-Ease—How you execute your experience and expert skills.

As a leader your brand can become known for the things that you do *with ease* that others find difficult. Consider it your *Expert-Ease*.

A group of Formula One[26] race drivers is gathered together for a test. They are each told to hold their hands either side of a measuring ruler and when the ruler is dropped they are to clap their hands together. Their reaction speed is recorded and compared between drivers. It is expected that the top drivers would have a faster reaction time than the slower drivers based upon their results over the years on the racetrack. The test results reveal something very interesting: *They all measure the same reaction time.*

But how can this be? Surely the better drivers have better natural skills or talents?

But no, all of them measured the same. The reason drivers were winning more races wasn't a faster reaction speed. It came down to how many hours they had spent behind the wheel and driving on particular race tracks. The winning drivers had better strategies and abilities to plan ahead, taking opportunities that other drivers didn't even see because they had simply spent more time on those circuits. The reason they won races had less to do with superior skills and everything to do with consistent and continual action, practice, and familiarity. Only after they had perfected their area of expertise could they try new things, innovate, and become heroes.

The drivers were winning more races not because their reflexes were faster than the others but because they had become so competent at driving that it was effortless. They had mastered the basics so well they could learn and develop new skills and then, over time and with practice, the newly learnt talents would become effortless, too.

---

[26] Formula One (also known as Formula 1 or F1) is the highest class of international racing for open-wheel single-seater formula racing cars sanctioned by the Fédération Internationale de l'Automobile (FIA). — https://en.wikipedia.org/wiki/Formula_One

Malcolm Gladwell[27] calls this *unconscious competence*. He suggests that if you do something well for 10,000 hours or more it becomes a natural talent and skill.

I'm at the wheel of the bright orange Datsun 180y. My hands grip the steering wheel in front of me and my palms are already sweaty. I can feel a drip of sweat go down my back and my forehead is beaded with it as I stare ahead at the front of the car. When I asked to learn to drive the car I was excited about the freedom it would give me. Living in the country there is no public transport and I dream that when I have my license I will be able to drive myself to my friends, to sports practice, to anywhere I want to go.

But now I am behind the wheel with my dad beside me in the passenger seat giving me instructions. I realise how incompetent I really am and how much there is to learn.

When you decide to become a leader in business, stepping out into your own brand or leading a franchise or taking on a leadership role, you can be excited about it but totally unaware of what is required. You are unconscious of your incompetence because you don't really know what it's going to take to lead, you just know you want to do it.

When you start out learning to lead you consider every step, much like being behind the wheel for the first time. Often you are unsure of yourself. You think first then act, going through manoeuvres slowly, carefully, and in a particular order. You have quickly become conscious of your incompetence and aware of your processes.

---

[27] Malcolm Gladwell is the author of five New York Times bestsellers — The Tipping Point, Blink, Outliers, What the Dog Saw, and David and Goliath. He is also the co-founder of Pushkin Industries, an audio content company that produces the podcasts Revisionist History, which reconsiders things both overlooked and misunderstood, and Broken Record, where he, Rick Rubin, and Bruce Headlam interview musicians across a wide range of genres. Gladwell has been included in the TIME 100 Most Influential People list and touted as one of Foreign Policy's Top Global Thinkers. — https://www.gladwellbooks.com/landing-page/about-malcolm-gladwell/

Eventually you become busy growing a business or becoming a leader. Just like getting your learner's license, you start to take shortcuts. You move from being a novice and you take a few more risks, putting your own spin on things. You are now consciously competent. You are driving your business or building your profile and you are planning, strategizing, and implementing.

After a few years running the business, being a leader has become second nature. You don't even think about half the stuff you do. Just like driving, you brake, change gear, accelerate, use the indicators, and check your mirrors (or at least we hope you do) without even planning to do so. It has become natural. You are now unconsciously competent.

If you have been in business or leading in your industry for a few years there are probably unique approaches and processes that you have forgotten you even do. You are operating on autopilot, just like driving home and not remembering how you got there. You have moved through the process from:

- unconscious incompetence, where you are totally unaware of what is needed to succeed

- to being conscious that you are incompetent and need to learn,

- through to conscious competence; doing something but being mindful of how you do it,

- to unconscious competence where you simply do things without even thinking about them.

If you are unconsciously competent, you have forgotten what you do with ease and the special insight, knowledge, or steps that create your Expert-Ease. It's also highly likely you have forgotten to tell your ideal audience about what you do really well naturally and what makes you the expert. If you think about it perhaps you have stopped pointing out what makes you the brand leader and what you do that can help them or how effortlessly you do what they find difficult.

DEVELOPING
YOUR
EXPERT-EASE

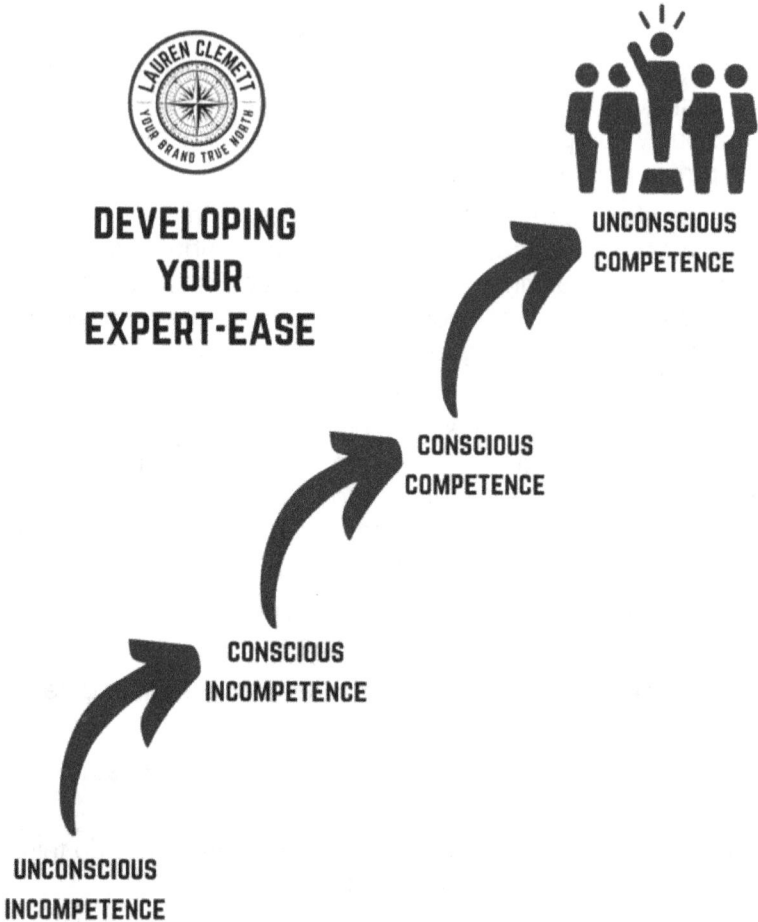

UNCONSCIOUS
COMPETENCE

CONSCIOUS
COMPETENCE

CONSCIOUS
INCOMPETENCE

UNCONSCIOUS
INCOMPETENCE

- So what makes you the expert?
- What do you do unconsciously because you've been doing it for years?
- What does your brand do with ease that others find difficult?
- What is your Expert-Ease?

- Have you created a unique process of approach you can use to stand out from the market?

Jason is struggling to position himself as the expert. For years he has worked on feature films like *Lord of the Rings* and he knows everything there is to know about videography. He has all the right equipment and knows how to set up the lighting and get the angles right. But all those skills are not helping him to attract clients. We discuss his process, what he does when he works with a client to create video to promote their business and their brand.

I ask him to write down what happens. He gets to step number 21 before he actually picks ups a video camera. We review the list and his Expert-Ease is right there in black and white. It takes more than half of his process to make sure the client feels at ease, working out the story they will tell in a two-minute video, how they will sit, what background or foreground would make the most impact. Everything he does is to help them create a great first impression.

Jason becomes a well-respected, sought-after videographer in the real estate industry. The properties he helps create marketing for sell quickly and at premium prices because he is telling stories effortlessly and captivating potential buyers with his videos.

Time for you to consider the steps you take that are your Expert-Ease.

Taking Steps

IF YOU TAKE the time you can probably list out your unique way of doing things as a numbered list of steps. Start at (1) and work through all the steps you take to accomplish a process and deliver a result. Go back and review every step. You may have added one step where in fact you do multiple things at that time. The devil is in the details. Remember your Expert-Ease are those things you do that you may have forgotten about.

If you have years of expertise you probably think everyone knows how to do what you do or how to deliver the services your business offers, but I challenge you to review.

- Real estate agent? Not everyone knows how to sell a house.
- Accountant? Not everyone knows how to complete a tax return.
- Fitness coach? Not everyone knows how to prepare a balanced meal and a workout plan.
- HR manager? Not everyone knows how to keep a team performing well.
- Business owner? Not everyone is prepared to take on that responsibility.
- Wellness practitioner? Not everyone knows how to stay healthy.

These may seem totally simple processes to you because you instantly know what to do. Why wouldn't you? You've been doing what you do for years and it's now natural instinct. And yes, people can learn to do what you do, they just don't have the time. The most valuable currency on the planet right now is time and people are prepared to pay to have a leader like you deliver results.

- If you can get someone to a better place in their life faster, they will ask you for help.

- If your skills can get the job done more quickly and better, they will pay you for that.
- If your decision-making skills are more experienced and proven, they will ask your advice.
- If you communicate, innovate, or get results in a way they can't, they will hire or promote you.

Even better if you have a unique way of doing something that relates back to your brand story. It makes it easy to stand out as the leader especially when there are loads of competition.

Sharon is a sales specialist but there are so many others who claim to do exactly the same thing. She knows her process will work, it did for years when she worked in corporate sales, but she is now the leader of her own business and without clients. How can she prove it?

She has a brand, but too many messages to try to explain her process. When she gets in front of a prospect they don't seem to connect with what she is saying. Her social media posts are going unnoticed. She has to find a way to cut through.

We talk about her childhood and the environment she grew up in. Her dad was the general manager of large department stores and instilled a sense of order in the household in the same way he inspired his teams at work to look after the customers. She knew she had to keep things organised, lining up the shoes on the porch and taking time to make sure her room was tidy.

She enjoyed lots of after-school activities and in order to keep things the way her dad liked them she developed systems. It is this ability to systemise even the most basic of chores that is her Expert-Ease. When it is applied to B2B sales processes and customer service she has a step-by-step process that is totally unique to her business and it will deliver results.

Sales 2 Success[28] has its brand promise. Sharon finds it easy to explain to prospects what makes her brand different. She can help them introduce sales systems that are perfect for their

---

[28] https://sales2success.com.au/

business, easy to maintain and duplicable to any sales team. We update her brand to include a tagline which communicates positivity, confidence, and better communicates the brand promise. Sharon goes on to win awards for her process and she builds a successful sales consultancy company.

One of the most known personal brands on Earth, Oprah Winfrey talks about how your purpose flows throughout your entire life. Watching her on stage at the Brisbane Convention Centre, sitting amongst hundreds of others who are there to learn from her stories and soak in some of her positive energy, one key phrase she says rings in my ears and connects with my heart. She says, "Purpose is the thread that connects everything you do that leads you to an extraordinary life." At just three years old Oprah was reading scripture at the front of her church. She grew up with a dream of becoming a journalist and TV presenter, and the rest is history.

Think back to when you were a child and what you loved to do. What came to you naturally? Regress for a moment and think about all the things you were naturally good at as a kid. What did you love to do, without even trying? Consider how your natural talents and your learnt skills have created a unique approach—that is your Expert-Ease.

BRAIN DUMP

GRAB A PACK of Post-it Notes[29], a pen, and the dining room table (a wall works well too), and brain dump of all the things you know about and the process you instinctively know how to do. No matter how minuscule or unimportant you think it is, write it down and slap it on the table or wall:

- Write what you know about or are naturally good at.
- Write the things you have experience in or knowledge of.
- Write the natural traits you have as well as the learnt skills.
- Write the outcomes you can deliver and the methods you use.
- Consider everything you have learnt over the years as well as the talents you were born with.
- Keep going until you have exhausted your brain and have all of your Expert-Ease points written on Post-it Notes all over the table or wall.
- Once you have emptied your brain out onto the Post-it Notes start arranging them into a process.
- Consider if you were to teach someone what you know, what would they want and need to know first?
- Then what would you teach them?
- Now what?

You can group the notes into sets of actions, learnings, or activities, filing them together into topics. For example, a fitness coach might start their process by the topic of goal-setting and have a number of steps for that part of the process. Another topic might be measurements and a bunch of Post-it Notes go together for that step, and so on.

---

[29] https://www.post-it.com/3M/en_US/post-it/

Write the name of each topic on a different coloured Post-it Note and put that at the top of the groups you have formed.

Step back and consider the process. Move topics around to make sure you have everything in the right order. Move Post-it Note steps from one group to another if you think it works better under another topic.

Develop a name for your process. Make it memorable and based on what your ideal client wants to achieve.

Create a Brand Platform from Your Expert-Ease

YOUR BRAND PLATFORM

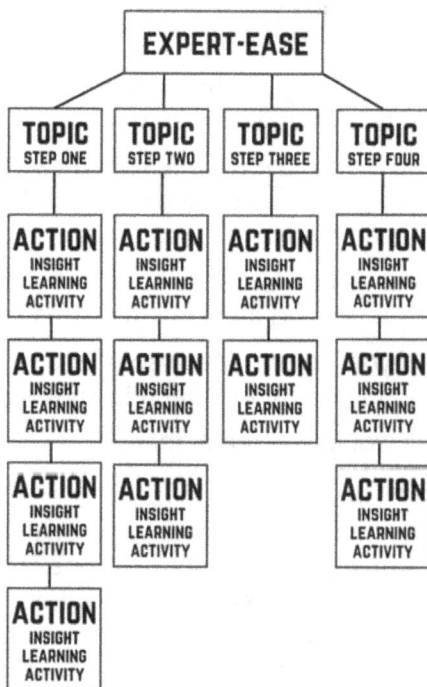

```
                    EXPERT-EASE

    TOPIC      TOPIC      TOPIC      TOPIC
    STEP ONE   STEP TWO   STEP THREE STEP FOUR

    ACTION     ACTION     ACTION     ACTION
    INSIGHT    INSIGHT    INSIGHT    INSIGHT
    LEARNING   LEARNING   LEARNING   LEARNING
    ACTIVITY   ACTIVITY   ACTIVITY   ACTIVITY

    ACTION     ACTION     ACTION     ACTION
    INSIGHT    INSIGHT    INSIGHT    INSIGHT
    LEARNING   LEARNING   LEARNING   LEARNING
    ACTIVITY   ACTIVITY   ACTIVITY   ACTIVITY

    ACTION     ACTION                ACTION
    INSIGHT    INSIGHT               INSIGHT
    LEARNING   LEARNING              LEARNING
    ACTIVITY   ACTIVITY              ACTIVITY

    ACTION
    INSIGHT
    LEARNING
    ACTIVITY
```

This—your Expert-Ease— is the foundation of your unique approach, the thing you do with ease, and the unique way you deliver outcomes, value, and expert services or quality products. From here you can now develop and even trademark your Expert-Ease and you can turn it into an entire platform to launch your brand. From this platform you can develop brand assets such as a book or a coaching program, your keynote presentation, or an entire business model or service delivery process.

You can certainly use your Expert-Ease to define your unique brand story—the reason behind what makes your brand, service or products so different, and easily explain what makes you a different leader. Don't panic if you feel your brain dump includes things you have learnt from others. Obviously, you do not want to plagiarise another's process. *Your approach* might not be totally new, it might just be an improvement on what already exists.

Frenchman Marcel Bich[xiii] first saw a ballpoint pen developed by Argentinian Lazlo Biro during World War II, and he decided to manufacture an affordable version using Swiss technology that created the tiny ball in the tip of the pen that enables the ink to flow freely without clogging. Marcel invested heavily in advertising, winning awards for his posters, and with a short catchy name, BIC helped shift the world from using fountain pens to ballpoint pens. Today, BIC is the best-selling pen in the world having sold its billionth pen in 2006. We bet you have one in your desk draw!

So your Expert-Ease might not be an innovation or something you invented. It can be the tiny details that you have improved upon to make something that already exists even better, more accessible, or more user-friendly.

Your handiwork in developing a different way of looking at something might be the very reason why people will want to choose you to lead them.

DRAW IT OUT

ROSS IS PACING his dining room, whiteboard marker in hand, looking down at his shoes as he walks back and forth. We have been working on his brand for a few hours and he feels he is going in circles. He is stuck, but I push him to keep reviewing his area of Expert-Ease. For years he has worked incredibly hard to be a leader in business, working within corporate organisations and contracting for service providers. Now as a business owner and consultant, he knows so much about what he does and he knows his Expert-Ease. But there are so any others who offer similar consulting services it is hard for him to define his point of difference.

What about all his experience in sales? Or the fact that he totally understands customer retention management systems (CRMs) and is partnered with a globally recognised platform? He loves talking about customer experience but so many others offer that already. There is so much more to what he knows and what he can do to help small to medium enterprises (SMEs), but how can he explain his Expert-Ease easily? What can he base his entire brand on that will align with his personal values, skills, and talents? How can his brand communicate his unique approach so his prospects instantly get it?

Ross has passion and purpose behind his desire to be known. He really wants to help people grow their businesses by being better at communicating with their existing clients. He sees so many SMEs waste time, effort, and money chasing new business when they could easily harvest sales from the customers they already have.

If they just knew how to communicate better, and if only he knew how to communicate that he is the one to help them do that.

As we discuss his area of expertise and his experience, Ross recalls a time when he took over a project for a struggling business after asking them the simplest of questions:

"When was the last time you spoke to your customers?"

The answer shocks him—"Never," they say.

He has helped so many companies like this turn around their cash flow, implementing simple systems to talk more regularly with their clients. It's so basic, so obvious, but he is appalled at how frequently he finds businesses not doing it. He knows that so many small businesses could be doing so much better if they had his help. But how can he explain that easily and in a way that people will value what he offers?

On the whiteboard in front of him, Ross begins to draw his process as a diagram as if he were leading a workshop and teaching what he knows. The diagram looks like a tree. Together we create the Client Orchardist approach. Ross develops a unique approach and process, sharing how a business doesn't need to keep growing more new trees, they can simply pluck the fruit off the branches of their existing trees to make money.

Nexttree Consulting is born. The brand story makes for easy explaining and Ross' consultancy becomes an SME solution many know, like, and trust. His expertise was always there, he just had to draw it out.

BUSINESS GROWTH CONSULTANCY

Realising Potential

Your brand can paint a picture of what your ideal prospects want and your brand story can give them everything they need to trust why you are the expert they need.

Still seeking out your expertise? Consider how you might draw it. What shapes or symbols could you use to explain it, like Ross's tree or Simon Sinek's Golden Circle? Your Expert-Ease might be in the palm of your hand. Still not sure where your expertise can be found? Put your hand up and take a look at your fingers:

Your Thumb

- What you are really good at, to the point that people complement you on being great at it?
- What do you do that's really, really good?
- What makes you feel good when you are doing it?
- What activities do you look forward to in your day?
- What are you doing when you really feel 'at ease,' like you were born to do it?

Your Index Finger or Pointer

- What do you know and could teach?
- What knowledge have you gathered over the years that can be a lesson for others?
- What skills did you qualify for and have you honed?
- What topics could you write or speak about for 30 minutes?
- If a journalist asked you for information as the expert in that area, what would it be?

Your Middle Finger

- What won't you do, don't you do, hate doing, and will never offer?
- What is the industry doing that you detest?
- What trait or activity really turns you off?
- What makes you angry and annoyed, that you would rather not have to deal with?

Your Ring Finger

- What are you really passionate about?
- What do you care about the most?
- What really engages you?
- What do you find yourself talking about in a social scene?
- What activity do you do that seems to take no time at all because you are so immersed in it?

Your Little Finger or Pinkie

- What are the little things you do really well?
- What are the seemingly insignificant but vital and important things you do?
- What natural traits were you born with that make it easy to be the expert?
- What details do you always cover off and identify when you work?
- What small things do you appreciate when others provide service to you?
- Can you use this insight to create a diagram that could easily be drawn on a whiteboard in a workshop to help people understand your process so well that they can replicate the drawing to others?

- Consider everyday shapes that a child or someone who doesn't feel very creative could do.

- Refine it to the simplest form and review how it fits with your brand promise and identity.

You now understand the benefit of being an expert and having an Expert-Ease that you can clearly communicate. Now it is time to define the value of your brand and how you can create a brand message that clearly communicates why you are a worthy leader worth paying for that expertise.

SOUTH

"Strive not to be a success,
but rather to be of value."

~ Albert Einstein

YOUR GREATEST ASSET

I'M SITTING AT my small wooden desk at the little country school that's perched on the hilltop above the valley where I live. I have my head down trying to look like I'm reading but the words aren't easy. Suddenly I notice the teacher is right there next to me, standing over my desk. What does he want? I shrivel into my chair trying to disappear but it's too late, he's bending down to speak to me. What does he want?

He crouches down and I slowly raise my eyes to meet his.

"Lauren," he quietly says, "I know you are having trouble reading and I don't think you are going to learn like the other children are."

My heart sinks. *Not another thing that makes me different.*

I'm already smaller than the others, have asthma, and am certainly not included among the popular kids in the playground. I don't need another thing that makes me unusual.

"I think you may have word blindness[30]," he says.

Now I'm intrigued. *What on earth is word blindness?*

You see, he was not the horrible teacher you imagine from a Pink Floyd music video, he was actually a very good teacher. He knew I was the kind of kid that if you told me there was something I couldn't do, it was going to drive me to prove you wrong!

Now, all I want to know is, *What I can do to fix this?*

---

[30] 'Word blindness' is an old-fashioned term used to mean that a person is unable to recognize and understand words that he sees. This was the term used to describe dyslexia when it was first described by doctors in the late 19th century. It means that the person does not seem to be able to remember the order and sequence of letters in a word from one time to the next. A child might be be drilled for hours on an easy word, but the next time he saw the word would not recognize it. —https://www.dyslexia.com/question/word-blindness/

As it turns out, *word blindness* or *dyslexia* is not something you can fix. It's something you work with and it's become my superpower. My greatest asset.

My teacher sets me a daily list of 10 words to learn, instructing me to close my eyes and imagine the shape of the word each time. He finds books with stories I love and I start to consume them like lollies. Over time I increase my vocabulary and I start to get it. When I finish school I get a report that Mr. Higgott writes, stating, "If we had a class full of Laurens there is no limit to how far we could go."

A balloon of pride still swells in my chest when I read this today.

Later in life I train as a graphic designer and work for studios providing services to advertising agencies, mixing colour and creating mock-ups for adverts well before desktop computers arrive on the scene. (In fact, I get to work on one of the first Apple Macs in New Zealand.) As a result of my ability to see the shape of words in my mind and the constant work colour-matching and recreating branded pieces for ads I become really good at knowing what brands look like.

When I eventually land roles at the big agencies as a production manager, working amongst creative teams at Saatchi & Saatchi, Ogilvy & Mather[31], Clemenger, and Grey Worldwide, I begin to be a bit of an insurance policy by checking artwork before it goes to print to make sure the logos and colours are

---

[31] Ogilvy & Mather . . . is one of the largest marketing communications companies in the world. Through its specialty units, the company provides a comprehensive range of marketing services including: advertising; public relations and public affairs; branding and identity; shopper and retail marketing; healthcare communications; direct, digital, promotion, relationship marketing. Ogilvy & Mather services Fortune Global 500 companies as well as local businesses through its network of more than 450 offices in 120 countries. — https://www.devex.com/organizations/ogilvy-and-mather-68563

right. Later, as the brand manager at AXA[32] I am able to easily communicate the brand promise to the marketing team. I help them leverage the brand through sponsorships. As a result, we create much higher brand awareness in the market.

After that I open my own agency and am able to effortlessly manage creatives, briefing them on what is needed and giving them ideal feedback on what meets the brief and what doesn't. We develop and deliver some amazing work for our clients.

A few years later I discover that what I was doing all this time was the science of neurobranding—understanding how the brain 'sees' brands. I Google a neurobranding specialist called Peter Steidl[33] and read his book. I contact him to see if he can recommend the best place to get a qualification in this field. After I explain my background he tells me I'd be better off as the lecturer, not the student! He advises me to simply keep doing what I am doing and be the leader in the space of personal branding, using neurobranding to help business leaders and entrepreneurs to position their unique brand to be seen and noticed.

In 2016, a colleague encourages me to enter the Stevie Awards[34] for my approach because I have helped so many

---

[32] Axa S.A. (styled as AXA) is a French multinational insurance company. The head office is in the 8th arrondissement of Paris, France. It also provides investment management and other financial services. — https://en.wikipedia.org/wiki/Axa

[33] Hello, I'm Peter Steidl. I am a business consultant, author and educator with decades of experience in more than 20 countries on five continents. My work brings me into contact with a wide range of people and organizations in both the private and public sectors. I also read widely – everything from business and marketing to neuroscience and evolutionary biology. — https://petersteidl.com/about/

[34] The Stevie® Awards are the world's premier business awards. They were created in 2002 to honor and generate public recognition of the achievements and positive contributions of organizations and working professionals worldwide. In short order the Stevie has become one of the world's most coveted prizes. There are eight Stevie Awards programs, each with its own focus, list of categories, and schedule. —https://stevieawards.com/about-stevie%C2%AE-awards

people get clear on their brand message, how they want to make people feel, and the perception they want to own in their industry, all by using neurobranding.

I am up against some large agencies but I win a Silver for the unique process I have developed, based on the years of using my dyslexia disability to understand how we interact with brands. Judges approve of my approach to branding development, making neurobranding insight available to business owners, entrepreneurs, and SMEs that is usually only accessible at large and expensive advertising agencies. I am using my dyslexia disability as my greatest asset, helping people paint the picture of their brand in the mind of their ideal audience, creating strong brand perception, and building brand profiles.

I set about creating a brand profile for myself and make all the same mistakes my clients have, creating logos that really don't align with my personal brand. One version of my branding includes an icon that looks like the wings Air Force pilots get. The font is even called 'Top Gun'.

More than one person sees my branding and asks if I had been a pilot or flown in the Air Force, and it concerns me. Other than my dashed hopes as a kid of becoming an air hostess when I grew up and my love of traveling the world, there is nothing in my background to even suggest I can fly, let alone pilot a plane. I certainly don't have my pilot's license, let alone the ability to fly a fighter jet, and I realize I am way off brand.

Thankfully I haven't gone too far down the collateral creation route and can rebrand quickly, and today my brand is 100 percent aligned with my own personal story of growing up in the bush and using a map and compass to find purpose, direction, and meaning.

The lesson it taught me is that not everyone considers the brand story when they start up a business. Those who do go on to create brands that have timeless and life-long appeal.

Michael Dransfield[35] is one of those. He begins working at Bespoke Jewellers in the U.K., polishing his skills and honing his craft. The jewellery brand is well-established and well-known but Michael moves to Australia and he has to start from scratch with no reputation and no known brand name.

As a quality jeweller who personally meets his clients and designs amazing unique rings tailored to their exact needs, he also delivers them at a price similar to the high street jewellery brands. Michael doesn't want to have a cheap brand. He wants his clients to feel like they are getting a top-quality established service they can trust. He struggles with the idea of simply using his name as the brand. So we work on a brand identity that would make his service look and feel established and quality, but accessible and special.

Michael loves designing engagement rings and the value he offers is that the proposal can be handled stress-free and totally uniquely, with the recipient of the ring knowing that no one else in the world has a ring like theirs.

My research discovers that one of the first recorded instances of someone proposing marriage with a diamond ring was the Archduke Maximilian of Austria who proposed to Mary of Burgundy in 1477[36]. The brand Burgundy Bespoke Jewellery is born and even though the business is new, the perception it communicates is that this is an established, quality brand that will treat you like royalty.

---

[35] Where it began… In 2004 I started Form Bespoke Jewellers in Leeds, West Yorkshire (UK) with Tim Swann. Noticing that there was a gap in the market for our expert skills and jewellery industry experience, we created Form Bespoke Jewellers to offer something unique for customers – a new way for people to buy fine jewellery. Moving to Australia… in 2011, I emigrated to Brisbane with my family. And .. Burgundy Bespoke Jewellers was born. — https://www.linkedin.com/in/michael-dransfield/?originalSubdomain=au, also https://burgundybespokejewellers.com.au/about/

[36] Who Had the First Diamond Engagement Ring? — https://www.engagementringbible.com/who-had-the-first-diamond-engagement-ring/

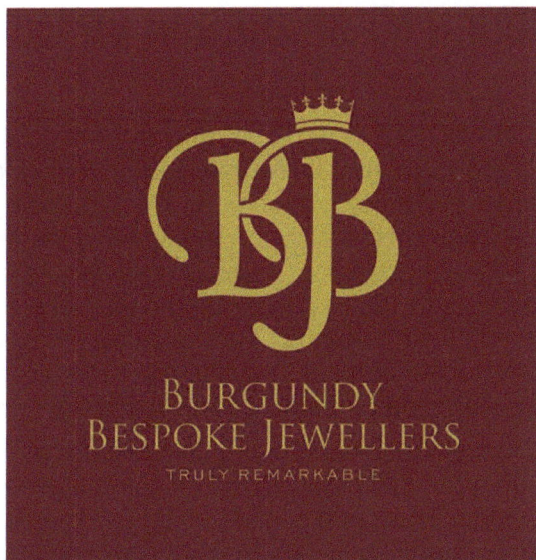

Now you know how your brand can paint the picture of the outcome and make potential customers and clients feel a certain way, even before they have engaged your services or bought your products. The major outcome for you is that you can apply neurobranding to both your personal and the business brand. You now know how to stand out and connect with your ideal prospects, instantly engaging them with more meaningful communication so they know and trust you will deliver the outcome they want, even before they work with you.

Let's dig into your brain to understand how neurobranding can impact the world around us and how you can use it to be seen and noticed by your ideal audience.

HIDDEN MESSAGES IN BRANDS

HAVE YOU SPANGLED your home recently? I'm sure you have a Spangler in the cupboard! Of course, you have no idea what I'm asking about but if the development of the vacuum cleaner had been any different, this certainly would have made sense to you. You see James Spangler[37] invented his 'electric suction sweeper' way back in 1907 to deal with the dust at his workplace that was aggravating his asthma. He shows his invention to his cousin, Susan Hoover and her husband sees the business opportunity, purchasing Spangler's patent, and the rest is history.

Today, 'Hoover' has become a *genericide*, a brand name which, through a gradual process, has become a generic word used by the world. The same goes for Frisbee, Thermos, or Band-Aid. Now, though, you can 'Hoover' anything. Kids 'hoover up their peas,' dogs 'Hoover their dinner.' The brand explains exactly what it does because it paints a picture of the outcome, just like telling someone to, 'Google it.' In reality, you could be using any search engine or device. We often 'Google' stuff on Siri. Of course, time is one way to achieve this as a brand.

Familiarity and consistent use of the brand name to describe an action is a great way to develop that 'ear worm' that makes its way into the brain and cements the perception of a leading brand. Brands also use visual clues to communicate directly with our brains.

It's incredibly hot in Chiang Mai, Northern Thailand, where we have been living for the past few months. Our final task before we head south is to order new drapes for our apartment back home.

---

[37] While working as a janitor at a department store in Canton, Ohio, James Murray Spangler invented a portable electric vacuum cleaner. The vacuum cleaner's design was upright, and it used a cloth bag to collect the dirt that was vacuumed up. Spangler first tested his invention in 1907 and patented it after a number of modifications in 1908. He founded the Electric Suction Sweeper Company to manufacture his design. — https://ohiohistorycentral.org/w/James_M._Spangler

We've been told the fabric makers here provide amazingly good quality at very affordable prices so we jump on 'Chocolate' and 'Cherry Cola,' the two trusty hired motor scooters, carefully ease our way out onto the busy road, and blast off into the dusty streets to find the warehouse. We keep up with the locals, zooming past the old stone walls of the city, alongside the canal, down a few narrow one-way alleys, and after a few wrong turns we eventually find our location. We park the scooters and hurry into the fresh coolness of the air conditioning inside the curtain shop.

We have brought the measurements from home scribbled on a piece of paper and thankfully the staff who speak limited English (which is still far better than our smattering of Thai) can understand and they proceed to help us find the colours and styles we want. Order placed, we zoom back home, hoping our curtains will fit and not hang a few inches off the ground when we get them home, thanks to something lost in translation.

A few weeks later they are ready to be collected and we zoom off once again on Chocolate and Cherry Cola, arriving at the factory to be warmly greeted by the smiling staff. We check the order and they look great. *Let's hope they fit back in our apartment in Australia.* But right now we have a different problem. The curtains are in a massive box that weighs a ton and won't possibly fit on a scooter. We Google the courier company nearest our accommodation. It's FedEx and we are relieved. We order a taxi and get back with our massive box of curtains. We know our treasured goods will make their way directly to our home on the Gold Coast of Australia and we know we can rely on fast and efficient service even though we have never used FedEx before.

Why do we feel this way about a brand we have no experience (at the time) using? What words would you describe the service you get from FedEx? Direct? Efficient? Speedy? Fast? How do you know this? Ever taken a close look at the FedEx logo? Did you ever notice there is a large white arrow in the logo? Go on, take a closer look between the E and the x:

See, it's been there all the time! No matter if you have experienced the FedEx service or not you know what the brand stands for because the logo has been telling your brain what the brand is all about. You know with FedEx that your parcel will get direct to its destination fast. The brand is telling you that, even if you have never actually used them to send something.

Now you will start looking more closely at brands won't you? Clever brands do this with visual pictures that the brain sees, absorbs and understands even before you buy from them. It's a science called *neurobranding* and it can cut through the noise and engage your prospect's brain to create a perception of your business in their hearts and minds.

- So what emotions or message is your brand communicating to your ideal clients and customers?
- How do you want your brand to make them feel?
- What instant opinion do you want them to have when they see your brand?

Brands can and do get it wrong (or right depending on how you look at it).

Queen's latest release blares from the stereo system as Mark continues to work on yet another album cover. Bent over the desk in the small flat, Mark is consumed by the art he creates. Mark has been commissioned to develop a brand for a U.K.-based fried chicken diner and, surrounded by the framed posters and artwork he has created for well-known works by U2, Gilles Peterson, Amy Winehouse, and Avicii, he has no idea the Dirty

Bird logo he designs will become a viral sensation as one of the most controversial logos of all time[xiv]. The brand owners insist the logo is simply a combination of the d and b of the brand name brought together to look like a chicken. They say all concept of the logo being phallic is 'in the eye of the beholder'. Of course their marketing continues to play on the brand strategy, with suggestive posters and headlines.

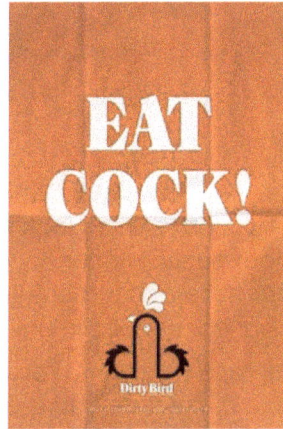

Is it wrong or is it clever use of neurobranding? Sometimes you do wonder if the graphic designer is playing a joke on the world.

The Department of Prime Minister and Cabinet in Australia have their internal team develop a new logo for the Women's Network[38] which works in with the current suite of logos. Unfortunately it is released to the public and is immediately mocked.

WOMEN'S
NETWORK

This is not a good look for a department already struggling with poor publicity over how it is handling women's issues. Another case of neurobranding gone wrong or an intentional jest by designers inside the government's departments?

Perhaps it's time to review the hidden messages in your brand to make sure you are communicating the right way?

On the long drive from New York to Seattle Jeff and his wife are enthusiastically discussing their plans. They are taking a big risk giving up a Wall Street lifestyle to capitalise on a new internet boom. But they have drive and ambition, and they are not going to regret missing out on this opportunity. In the car they formulate a business plan. They consider the flow of merchandise and how they can create a better customer experience and what products they will start selling. They know that even if they get it right just about anyone can copy them because in the 90s e-commerce is the new frontier and there are virtually no rules.

They excitedly toss about ideas for brand names considering 'Relentless' as a good name to try (Jeff still owns the URL to this day, go on, check it out and see where it takes you), however they settle on another name, Amazon[xv]. Exotic and different, it is the name of the biggest river in the world, just as they plan to make their online store the biggest bookstore in the world. Jeff also likes that the name begins with 'A,' and will appear at the top of an alphabetised list.

Amazon started with books but now they sell everything from A to Z and they ship almost anywhere in the world. The brand is all about providing a happy customer experience, making it easy to shop online for anything you need. Before long everyone buys everything on Amazon, especially in the U.S.

Take a look at their logo to understand why so many people trust this brand.

amazon

See, there is an arrow from the A to the Z and the arrow also looks like a smile. And it's yellow, the colour of spontaneity, happiness, and fun. The black logo is the colour of authority and leadership. Something to be trusted, especially with your credit card details.

Your brand can convey your value. And it can paint a picture of the outcome no matter what that outcome may be, making your brand even more valuable than the business itself. With the right brand name you can create the right brand perception and people value you even if you start selling different services or products. A good brand name will last the test of time and enable your business to expand, contract, or adapt. A timeless brand grows with the business.

Maybe you are now looking at your business card or website and wondering, *Does my brand give the right message?*

You might even be considering a rebrand.

REBRANDING

ON A CRISP winter morning the sun is shining low in the blue morning sky and there is dew on the grass surrounding the golf course clubrooms. New to Australia, I am attending lots of networking events for business owners, getting to know the locals and building my personal brand reputation. With my brand-new business cards in my pocket and a hot tea in my hand, I hesitantly invite myself to join a small circle of suit-wearing entrepreneurs who are excitedly chatting about the weekend's sporting events.

I smile politely and sip my tea while listening in on the discussion, waiting for the right time to introduce myself. But before I find my way into the conversation a bright-eyed blonde next to me turns and offers her hand in greeting. We exchange names and get chatting. She lives locally and sells insurance, potentially an ideal client for me as I know it's difficult to stand out in that industry and she may be looking to build a profile. So I keep asking her more questions. We exchange cards and as my eyes read over her details they come to rest on the company logo and I can't help myself. I ask her, "Do you ever have difficulty with people thinking your business does something other than insurance?"

She laughs out loud and nods. "Yes, of course," she says, "all the time!" The others in the group have taken notice of our exchange, so she continues and regales everyone with her story.

Good people to know.

"Just last week." She says, "someone stopped me in the street and asked me about the WIFI signal issues they had on their phone. They saw the logo on my car door and assumed it was a WIFI internet company, not Western Farmers Insurance. And a week before that," she continues, "I had a call from an older gentleman who insisted I go to his house to assist him even though I quite clearly told him that all his issues could be sorted over the phone. On arriving at the man's house, I discovered he in fact had a problem with his internet, and he didn't need insurance."

We all laughed.

I ask her, "Has your company thought about changing the logo or rebranding?"

"I agree it's a problem," she said, "and even the tagline doesn't help matters."

But even today, if you go to the company website, the branding is exactly the same. It's a great example of how acronyms for brand names aren't always ideal. Perhaps this brand is betting on picking up a few potential clients who have simply got internet issues and might, on the off-chance, need insurance? But what a waste of their agents' time. Why would you continue to confuse the market?

We know Western Farmers Insurance[xvi] was around well before the internet (they founded in 1919), but sticking to their guns while a new technology has created a word that looks distinctly like their brand (WIFI) and has far wider use than their brand name probably means it's time to consider a rebrand.

So when should you rebrand?

Trying something new or refreshing your brand can be a pretty big deal and a step not to be taken lightly. A number of well-known global brands failed miserably at relaunching their brands including GAP[39] who rebranded during a busy Christmas period in 2010, ditching the instantly recognisable logo that had served the brand for more than 20 years and launching a new logo design with no warning. The original GAP brand disappeared without trace only to be brought back just a few short days after customers rebelled.

New Coke was a similar rebranding debacle when executives decided the iconic flavoured beverage needed a refresh and changed the hundred-year-old recipe in response to the market share Pepsi was winning with its New Generation advertising campaign. Consumers hated it and clever PR by Pepsi suggested Coke was trying to make its product more Pepsi-like. The New Coke product lasted only months before the old product was brought back. Coke learnt the lesson that nostalgia and loyalty count for plenty in a highly competitive market. And Pepsi? Well they have struggled to retain their sense of brand identity too, spending billions on updating their look numerous times over the years.

So why rebrand if it's so problematic?

If your brand uses a name, phrase, or letters that have changed in meaning or stand for something that has become general use in language, such as LOL, OMG, or WIFI (in the case of Western Farmers Insurance), it's probably time to rebrand and ensure you are not confusing the marketplace. If you have a competing brand that gives you grief or if you own a business that may have outgrown its brand because it has pivoted in a different direction and the brand is no longer serving

---

[39] The Gap, Inc., commonly known as Gap Inc. or Gap (stylized as GAP), is an American worldwide clothing and accessories retailer. Gap was founded in 1969 by Donald Fisher and Doris F. Fisher and is headquartered in San Francisco, California. The company operates six primary divisions: Gap (the namesake banner), Banana Republic, Old Navy, Intermix, Athleta, and Janie and Jack. Gap Inc. is the largest specialty retailer in the United States, and is 3rd in total international locations, behind Inditex Group and H&M. As of September 2008, the company has approximately 135,000 employees and operates 3,727 stores worldwide, of which 2,406 are located in the U.S. — https://en.wikipedia.org/wiki/Gap_Inc.

the business, this is a good sign that change probably needs to occur.

And don't worry about how long the brand has been around. EFM Fitness has been around a long time, but now has a competitor on the scene, EMF Fitness. The new brand is gaining momentum but the original gym doesn't want to change their name, because, "We were here first." It will be interesting to see who wins.

I believe it would be better to move away from an acronym and create a brand name that means something, and who cares how long you have been in the market? Consumers only care about themselves and they live in the here and now.

Rebranding is often necessary when a brand has been developed poorly or without a long-term strategy. Sometimes the brand was an afterthought when the company was created. This is often the case when the business creators underestimate the power of a brand or choose initials or founders' names as their brand name. Dysfunctional branding is the major reason behind the need for rebrands, and they can be mammoth efforts with a massive scope of change affecting everything from company structure and processes to costly signage, vehicles, uniforms, and marketing to be updated.

But sometimes rebrands are not only necessary, they are good for brands.

On a hot summer's day Ajay is standing in the stuffy back office of the small stationery store. He scratches his head wondering what on earth has possessed him to buy this business. Surrounded by packed shelves of products, overflowing with boxes and bags of all shapes and sizes, filled with paper, pens, clips, binders, folders, staplers, ink cartridges, what is he going to do?

He knows the business has loyal clients, local offices, and schools who purchase regularly, but every time the staff pick up the phone they have to explain what the business *doesn't* do.

How many times has someone this week asked about buying a photocopier?

He looks up at the sign on the window eyeballing the E at the end of the brand name that has clearly and boldly been underlined in a desperate attempt to differentiate the brand from another much larger Japanese electronics brand. His gut tells him he will have to change the name, but a nagging fear creeps into his mind over and over again. *What if we change the name and clients don't like it or worse, they start buying their stationery from someone else?*

Ajay contacts me and we begin discussing how he can better communicate the difference between Sharpe Office Supplies and the Sharp Corporation[40] in Japan. We overcome his fears and rebrand the business as Ezi Office Supplies based on their core value of making their clients lives easier. The logo looks like a Post-it Note, exactly what most receptionists use to remind themselves of the stationery needed on the next order. Post-it Notes are what office workers put on the Sharp photocopier to alert the office manager that it is out of paper or low on toner.

sharpeoffice
Stationery Supply Solutions

Ezi Office Supplies
Getting On With Business

---

[40] Sharp Corporation is a Japanese multinational corporation that designs and manufactures electronic products, headquartered in Sakai-ku, Sakai, Osaka Prefecture. Since 2016 it has been majority owned by the Taiwan-based Foxconn Group. Sharp employs more than 50,000 people worldwide. The company was founded in September 1912 in Tokyo and takes its name from one of its founder's first Ever-Sharp mechanical pencil, which was invented by Tokuji Hayakawa in 1915. —https://en.wikipedia.org/wiki/Sharp_Corporation

Within months and despite Ajay's fears, the staff are answering calls using the brand as a genericide. Instead of saying, "No problem," they say, "That's Ezi!" Customers love it, and Ajay has to move the business into bigger premises less than a year later. They have now expanded into three stores.

Another successful rebrand is the logo with the iconic rings of Audi automobiles[xvii] which enabled a heavily structured merging of four different companies, each with their own history.

Audi

One of those four companies started as a bicycle maker and evolved over time to manufacture cars. They, like the other three businesses, hit financial trouble in the recession of 1929. All four (effortlessly) became one to not only modernise the business and create an instantly recognisable iconic brand, but it also helps them to defeat the Olympic Committee which tries to sue them for the use of rings in their logo[41].

Brian Chesky is in L.A. and Joe Gebbia lives in San Fransisco. Ches and Joe have kept in touch since design school, and they still find themselves talking about how much they hate their jobs in design firms. They bat around potential business ideas together. Joe's landlord raises the rent and his roommates move out, so Ches decides to move in with him. They still cannot afford the rent, but there is a third bedroom they do not use. As designers they know there is a conference coming up where there will be loads of students like them attending who can't

---

[41] https://didyouknowcars.com/history-of-the-audi-emblem/

afford hotels, so they grab three airbeds from storage, blow them up, and start promoting the Airbed & Breakfast concept.

Within days they have rented the beds for $80 and their idea has sparked an interest amongst creative millennials. A year later the AirBed & Breakfast website has 10,000 users and 2,500 listings from people looking to rent out temporary lodging. In March that same year the name of the company is shortened to airbnb[xviii]. Airbnb has now created an entirely new language with its meaningful iconography combining people, place, and love, moving away from a simple brand name to an icon everyone can instantly recognise.

MasterCard is another example of a rebrand getting it right, simplifying its identity after 50 years because consumers no longer need to see the brand name smeared across the advertising. Mastercard branding has now joined the ranks of Apple, Target, and Nike. Their distinctive combined red and yellow circles alone are enough for us to recognise their brand, and their brand name has disappeared almost entirely from their 'priceless' advertising campaigns.

Google and Instagram have also successfully rebranded, creating identities that resonate and move with the consumer's view of their brands and what their businesses stand for.

Here is some advice when it comes to considering neurobranding before deciding if you should even go ahead with a rebrand:

Be 100 percent clear on the reason for the rebrand.

- Is there a need for your brand to change?
- Has your business model changed?
- Have you merged or restructured how you deliver?
- Has the market indicated a new direction is needed?
- Is your current brand no longer communicating what you need it to do?

- Or is it a case of your executives getting bored with the current logo? Or maybe a change in leadership or agency that has led to a rebranding discussion?

Before you jump into what could be a costly exercise consider your customer and the brand loyalty they have. How will a rebrand affect them?

No one likes change.

Our human brains want to keep us safe and many brands who resist change count the cost when they become irrelevant, old fashioned, and disregarded or overtaken by more relevant brands. Certain traditional retail brands urgently need to rebrand to keep pace with the fast-moving online purchasing world, such as:

- Myers
- David Jones
- Walmart
- Debenhams
- Kircaldie

The longer they delay, the more stale their brands get, and consumers will move on for convenience and ease, which is why brands such as Uber Eats[42] are taking off.

If you know your brand is not speaking for your business or your business or consumer behaviour has fundamentally changed since you first developed your brand, you now have to communicate an entirely new proposition and you probably need a rebrand.

---

[42] Uber Eats is an online food ordering and delivery platform launched by Uber in 2014. Users can read menus, reviews and ratings, order, and pay for food from participating restaurants using an application on the iOS or Android platforms, or through a web browser. —https://en.wikipedia.org/wiki/Uber_Eats

Branding is way more than a logo.

A rebrand is far more than just changing your logo or updating to a new font or creating a new look. Your brand communicates the core and essence of your business, its values and key sales proposition. A rebrand needs to be considered from every angle of the business, from manufacture to marketing, customer service and sales to packaging and retail. Remember to work with your consumers and your team to convey the rebrand. You will need them to help tell the brand story, so involve them in the rebranding process and they will feel they are along for the journey.

Communicate the reasons behind the rebrand, show the evolution, and don't just change the logo. Change your approach, systems, and tone of your marketing as well and remember, no one likes change, so share your rebrand story to help explain why you are doing it.

How do you avoid a rebrand.?

The simple answer is to get 100 percent clear on what you want your brand to achieve from the outset.

Understand the target avatars, demographics, and psychographics and how you want your brand to make people *feel*. Consider your business plan and SWOT analysis (strengths, weaknesses, opportunities, and threats) and create a brand that will last the test of time and any change in technology, language, or consumer demand. Have a clear brief for your brand, create meaning and purpose in the look and feel, identify the underlying themes, emotions, and messages you want to convey about your brand and business.

If you invest in your brand from the outset you will probably never have to go through the pain of a rebrand.

BRAND VALUE

NOW THAT YOU KNOW about the power of a brand and how it can paint a picture in the mind of your ideal client, go on and draw a line through the S of South and turn it into a $ because South stands for *Value*. Value is more than what you get paid or the price of your goods and services. Value is all about what you deliver to your clients and customers that they value the most. You need to know what drives their needs and desires most.

The amygdala inside our brain is there to keep us safe and it sends messages to the prefrontal cortex to evaluate what we should do. Both fear and desire drive our decision-making. You may wonder if is it better to use fear tactics (a stick) or driving desire (a carrot) in your marketing but this is actually a moot point. The answer is *both* work.

Humans are weird. We make decisions based on emotions and non-tangible feelings, desires, and fears, which are all measured at the same time. We move away from pain, but often only if the pain of moving away is less than the pain of staying, which is why banks and internet providers have such loyalty. They make it harder to leave than to stay, even if you dislike the brand.

You need to ensure your brand speaks to the perceived and the real value it delivers. This is called the *brand promise*.

So what does your brand promise to deliver?

What is the outcome your ideal customer or client wants to achieve most?

Consider being a PRO:

- Problem
- Resolution
- Outcome

We have already discussed the **problem** you solve in WEST and the **resolution** you provide in EAST. In SOUTH it's all about painting a picture of the **outcome:**

- Problem (WEST)
- Resolution (EAST)
- Outcome (SOUTH)

So let's play with your brain to show you just how fast your customers will paint a picture of the outcome that your brand and business will deliver in order to value you and your leadership.

Your brain doesn't work in words, it works with pictures. Relax and concentrate on the two words on the following page, then allow your brain to do what it does naturally...

(Turn the page to see the two words…)

LAUREN CLEMETT

BACON & EGGS

What image did your brain create when you read those words?

- Some see fried eggs, others scrambled or poached.
- Some see bacon sizzling in a pan or on a plate with a cup of coffee next to it, perhaps even the morning paper.
- Many see a pig or a chicken.
- Most of us are just hungry at this stage and have started salivating for breakfast!

The thing is, you only got two words to read. You were not told anything more about them.

I didn't ask you to cook them.

I didn't ask you for the origins story.

I didn't tell you to serve them upon a plate.

Your brain, in milli-seconds, painted a picture of the outcome *you* wanted. So, realise this:

If you are not painting a picture of the outcome your brand delivers to your clients and customers they are making up their own minds about the value you are offering.

People want to see where your brand will take them, how you will help them and change their lives or get from where they are to where they want to be. Consider the images you want to create in the minds of your ideal audience, how you want them to see your brand and what you want them to trust you the most to deliver.

- What does your brand promise to deliver?
- Are you capable of delivering on that promise?
- What outcome does your ideal client or customer want the most?

Still unsure? Go back to WEST and redline your target avatar, really get into their shoes and walk up that mountain.

- Does your brand paint the right picture?
- Are you in fact painting too many pictures?

Inconsistency will devalue the trust people have in your brand. Remember the foot and finger exercises from WEST? The human brain likes what it knows, not what is new. So if you are sending out mixed messages you are confusing the marketplace and creating fear. Perhaps it's time to review your brand message, your website, and your marketing to ensure it is aligned and clearly communicating what you do and why you are the expert at it.

Albert Einstein once said, "Strive not to be a success, but rather to be of value," so find the value. Work out what images best paint the picture of success for your brand.

One of the best ways to make sure your brand stays consistent with its messages and delivers the brand promise is to create a mood board (explained in the next section) and ensure that you and your team refer to it when they are developing marketing, promotions, collateral, or sales pieces.

IN THE MOOD BOARD

BY NOW YOU have probably worked out that branding is an emotional and reactive way of getting into the mind of your ideal client and being recalled, remembered, and referred to with ease. The key word here is *emotion*. Humans buy with emotion and justify with fact. Even the Owls amongst us tend to make their final decisions after weighing up all the options and reading all the data before going with what feels right. We use our gut instincts to make lots of decisions, especially when it comes to purchasing services or products or following a particular leadership style.

For years branding agencies have used a tool to help them and their creative teams effortlessly slip into a brand's emotional presence and psyche, putting them in the mood of the brand before they put ideas on paper. This is especially important when you are dealing with multiple brands because you don't want to get confused when you are creating marketing or promotions and have the emotions of one brand cross over into the next.

Having a Mood Board is a great way to keep you on-brand with any of your marketing messages, website, collateral, or advertising, and it can even help your call centre teams and front of house staff to understand how to make customers feel. Architects and designers use mood boards to help convey and communicate the theme they are going for with the design of buildings and interiors. It helps everyone get on the same page and helps them understand why things are being done a certain way.

A mood board can be exactly that, a strong piece of card or board with images, colours, words, diagrams, designs, icons, styles, even textures, samples, or physical objects attached to it.

You can also use electronic versions of a mood board. Canva[43] has templates or you can use PowerPoint or even Pinterest to create one.

Today, it's really easy to create a brand mood board. You can make a physical one by cutting images out of magazines. Do not confuse a *mood board*, however, with a *dream board,* because the purpose of the mood board is not what you wish for, it is to encapsulate how you can communicate the emotion and feel of your brand.

Simply consider what your brand stands for and how you want to make people feel. (You may wish to wait to complete your mood board after you've completed your Brand True North and have selected your brand One Word.) Consider the examples of neurobranding I've shared so far. What colours, shapes or images quickly convey the emotion you want your brand to have the most? Then go looking for images, words, quotes, idioms, symbols, icons, and so on that communicate this feeling.

Once you have made your board keep it somewhere you can easily access it. You might even print it off and put it on the wall so you can refer to it and easily get 'in the mood' of your brand whenever you are creating any marketing content. It will help you use the right images, words, and phrases that fit with your brand core message.

You can even use a mood board as part of your marketing collateral. In 1996 while I was working at Saatchi & Saatchi, the Bank of New South Wales merged with TrustBank to create New

---

[43] Canva is an Australian graphic design platform, used to create social media graphics, presentations, posters, documents and other visual content.[4][5][6] The app includes templates for users to use. The platform is free to use and offers paid subscriptions such as Canva Pro and Canva for Enterprise for additional functionality.[7] The subscription price for Canva Pro is $119.40 per year for up to 5 people. Canva Pro can be provided to nonprofit organizations for free if they meet the guidelines. The subscription price for Canva for Enterprise is $30 per month per person.[8] In 2021, Canva launched a video editing tool.[9] Users can also pay for physical products to be printed and shipped. —https://en.wikipedia.org/wiki/Canva

Zealand's largest bank, Westpac[xix], and they needed a new brand look and feel. A traditional artist was commissioned create a work that incorporated 'Westpac red' to serve as the basis for the visual identity for the new brand. The artist, Hone Papita Raukura (Ralph) Hotere[44], did exactly that and his incredible work, "RED X2,[45]" with bold colour, brush strokes, and swirls of paint was scanned at high resolution. Then the painting itself was the mood board and it was used to brand, via colour and texture, all of the bank branches, ATMs, credit cards and advertising. The painting was the brand's mood board and it provided a consistent message (by either using it in its entirety or just a range of areas from the same palette). It now hangs in the Auckland Art Gallery (https://www.aucklandartgallery.com/).

Westpac Bank logo

You don't need to be a big bank to be able to do this.

---

[44] Hone Papita Raukura "Ralph" Hotere ONZ (11 August 1931 – 24 February 2013) was a New Zealand artist of Māori descent (Te Aupōuri and Te Rarawa). He was born in Mitimiti, Northland and is widely regarded as one of New Zealand's most important artists. In 1994 he was awarded an honorary doctorate from the University of Otago and in 2003 received an Icon Award from the Arts Foundation of New Zealand. — https://en.wikipedia.org/wiki/Ralph_Hotere

[45] Ralph Hotere's giant canvas, RED X2, stands in the foyer near a Maui carving on a 4000-year-old log, which is entwined with fibre-optic cabling to represent the past and the present. Both are giants: the painting is 3m by 2.4m and carving is two levels high, viewed as visitors ride the escalator from the ground floor to the main entry foyer on level one. Welcome to Westpac NZ's new national headquarters, spanning two buildings in Cooper and Company's $1 billion Britomart Precinct. —https://www.nzherald.co.nz/business/plush-offices-for-bank-staff-in-hq-move-video/CTMQXPOGVUPPBRTERJU4EWKA2U/

Engineering firm Arthur D. Riley[46] (ADR), established in 1909, wanted to modernise their brand and better communicate everything they had developed in their many years in business. As account manager at the Pivotal agency, I helped them create a mood board in a similar way to Westpac, with the designer blending a collage of elements that communicated the range of services the company provided using base elements of water, lightening, clouds, data, and so on.

From this concept we created a tagline that encompassed everything they did to test their innovations in the field before they released it for their clients to use: "Fieldsmart Technology." The mood board was used in its entirety on occasion and we would select small strips or parts of the mood board and use it as a background on collateral and on their website, vehicles, adverts, print mags etc.

So take your time and develop a mood board for your brand. It can be the perfect tool to help you easily paint the picture of the outcome each and every time someone interacts with your brand.

And now you are probably wondering, *What colour best communicates the emotion I want people to feel when they interact with my brand?* Time to go even deeper into the brain to understand how we 'see' colours and how we react to them, so you can choose the best combination for your brand identity.

---

[46] https://www.adriley.co.nz/

BRAND COLOUR

THE BRAIN MAKES decisions based on feelings and emotions and by now you know that we buy instinctively and justify purchases with facts. Brands can make us feel a certain way simply by using colour to create an emotional and also a physiological reaction. If you know how you want your brand to make people feel you can choose the right colours for your identity, marketing, packaging, online presence, and logo so your ideal client feels something when they interact with your brand. You can also better understand why people behave a certain way when they are part of your brand community or culture.

Although the eye is one of the most complex structures in the body (and it's this organ that sees colour) it's your brain that interprets it. We see colour in three bands—red, green, and blue—the same as a TV or computer screen does, and our brain's synapses interpret what we see, sending messages to our nervous system that evoke an emotional response.

Often these responses are instantaneous, creating a desire or repulsion well before any rational decision is processed. Blue, chocolate, or purple tomato sauce would cause most consumers to turn their nose up, whereas a white yoghurt or a brown burgers are highly acceptable.

Brighter colours have been tested to have a more positive response than pastel or muddy hues. Medical research has shown that the brain can be affected by colour to cause consumers to take action, increase concentration, or become more spontaneous or creative. There are even physical reactions to colour. Your heart rate, metabolism, appetite, and especially your mood all react to colour.

Studies have shown that individual colour preference affects brand purchase decisions and it's well known that cultural factors place different meanings on colours. For example, white in most

Western cultures indicates purity and faith, whereas Asian cultures treat white as the colour of death and suspicion.

The following information is based on Western cultural society and the deeply rooted emotional response to colour that occurs in Australasian, European, and American cultures.

Yellow

Yellow is the colour of sunshine—happiness, joy, warmth, and optimism. Yellow stimulates mental activity and is often associated with food brands. It is also the colour of spontaneity and impulsive behaviour and is often used with cheaper-priced products which require less of a decision-making process.

It is a bright, attention-getting colour, especially when put alongside another strong colour. Research has shown that if yellow is overused it can cause a nauseating effect and a disturbing influence. For example, babies sleep less and cry more in yellow painted bedrooms.

Yellow can also be the colour of warning. Black and yellow is often used on danger signs and in nature it is the colour of the bumble bee, a warning that a sting is in the tail and to take caution.

Dull Yellow indicates decay, sickness, cowardice, and should be avoided.

The gold spectrum of yellow can indicate prestige and wealth. Bling! If you have a high quality product you might want to add gold highlights as Harrods and John Deere do.

JOHN DEERE

Yellow is also a difficult colour to reproduce and fades fast in sunlight. As a brand manager it was always the yellow brands that were the most difficult to keep consistent across all media.

Yellow will disappear into a white background making it hard for your prospects to notice it.

A yellow brand will need a dark colour to highlight it.

Yellow: happiness, spontaneity, fun, joy, warmth.

Orange

Orange brands are energetic, enthusiastic, active and creative. Orange is a hot colour conveying warmth, excitement and energy. It is often used by energy or power companies.

The colour orange increases oxygen supply to the brain and stimulates appetite which is why confectionary and soft drink brands use it. Who can miss the bright orange of Fanta? Thanks to Fanta, orange is now associated with high-energy, sugariness.

Orange is also used for entertainment, sports, and cartoon brands because it is highly accepted by a younger audience and conveys excitement, such as Foxtel, Nickelodeon, Soundcloud.

Orange represents frivolity and abundance and shouldn't be used for brands that wish to convey seriousness, stability, or calmness.

Go on, buy it on your Mastercard, get it on Alibaba!

Dark orange can mean deceit and distrust.

Red-orange corresponds to desire, sexual passion, pleasure, domination, aggression, and thirst for action.

Gold evokes the feeling of prestige. The meaning of gold is illumination, wisdom, and wealth. It symbolises high quality.

Orange: energy, excitement, entertainment!

Red

Red is an emotionally intense colour. It can enhance human metabolism, increase respiration rate, and raise blood pressure. Red grabs attention and gives you the impression that time is passing faster than it actually is, creating urgency. It is the colour of fire and blood, power, determination, stimulation, desire, strength, and love. It is a high-octane and action colour, often used with energy drinks, games, sports, and car brands, such as Virgin, KFC, LEGO, Coca-Cola. It demands attention and is used with stop signs, traffic lights, and fire services and equipment to ensure they stand out.

Red stimulates people to make emotional decisions and is the perfect colour for 'Buy Now' or 'Click Here' buttons on websites.

It is also the colour of courage and is often used in nations' flags.

Red is often used in advertising to evoke erotic feelings (red lips, red nails, red dress). It is a bright, attention-grabbing colour, especially when put alongside another strong colour.

Light red represents joy, passion, sensitivity, and love.

Pink conveys romance and friendship with feminine emotions and passiveness.

Dark red is associated with willpower, rage, anger, leadership, courage, and vigour.

Reddish-brown is earthy and supportive, often associated with harvest or autumn.

Red: passion, drive, strength, power.

Brown

Brown is the colour of the earth, it is honest and genuine. Brown inspires stability and comfort, depth and neutrality. It is a very practical colour. It can communicate a natural roughness, although when mixed with cream or gold it can inspire elegant handmade quality, as with UGG boots, YSL handbags.

It has a richness often used for chocolate, wine, or coffee brands, such as Nescafe, Gloria Jeans.

When used for legal logos it indicates simplicity and frugal moderation.

Brown creates a feeling of warmth and can indicate a safe haven, often associated with wholesome or comfort foods like M&Ms, Nestle, Hershey's.

Being such a practical, down-to-earth, sensible colour it can also be seen as dull, boring, lacking sophistication, or humour.

Brown suppresses emotions and suggests stability and indicates masculine qualities, often used for earthmoving, landscaping, or construction brands because it indicates hardworking durability and sustainability.

Brown is non-emotive and calm, often used for comfort foods and products that create warmth and homeliness.

Brown product brands appear more durable and wholesome so use brown to indicate simplicity, seriousness, and practicality. UPS doesn't inspire you to get excited, it makes you feel they simply do their job.

Brown is organised and orderly, ideal for systems-focused brands.

Brown is not the life of the party, it is a reliable, safe refuge.

Purple

Purple is a colour associated with royalty because it is incredibly difficult to make purple dye, and in history any cloth that was made this colour was put aside for special purposes only. Purple conveys luxury, extravagance, glamour, wealth, service, and ambition.

The smoothness of Cadbury chocolate or smoking a Silk Cut cigarette. It is a great colour for brands that wish to convey quality, luxury, superior service or exclusivity and attainment. Cadbury and Silk Cut Cigarettes both famously use simple purple images often with little else in their advertising.

Research shows that purple is a favourite colour for the youth market with almost 75 percent of children preferring purple to all the other colours. This might explain why chocolate and toy packaging often has purple colouring.

Maybe this is why kids love Barney the Dinosaur?

Purple is a very rare colour in nature. Consumers may even consider it to be artificial, so although it might work for chocolate brands you may think twice about associating it with fresh or organic/natural food products.

Purple is also associated with wisdom, dignity, independence, healing, mystery, and magic.

Light purple is often chosen for feminine products and services because of romantic and nostalgic emotions (women's gym brands).

Dark purple evokes gloom and sad emotions and can cause impatience and frustration.

Purple: luxury, service, protection, mystery.

Green

Green is the colour of nature. It inspires emotions of growth, harmony, freshness, renewal, and restoration. BP uses this to advantage. Green is also a safe colour—a green light, a green tick, or environmentally-friendly products. Many medical brands package their products in green boxes or have green on the tube to help communicate the medicine is good for you. Often it is used to advertise medical products and services and is a favourite for ecological, conservation, agricultural, as well as spa/retreat ,and natural food brands, such as Green Giant, Woolworths, Starbucks.

Green can be associated with money and wealth but can also indicate ambition, greed, and jealousy. It can also indicate youth, inexperience, or naivety (green ski routes are the easiest).

It is a restful colour for human eyes. Many media companies will use a 'green room' for guests to relax in before they are interviewed. The walls are actually green!

Green also suggests endurance, perseverance, and steadiness.

Bright green is often used with a black background to stand out (Xbox)

Dull or dark green is commonly associated with money, the financial world, and Wall Street.

Yellow-green can indicate sickness.

Aqua green is associated with emotional healing and protection.

Olive green is the traditional colour of peace.

Green: nourish, nature, fresh, clean, environmentally friendly.

Blue

Blue is the colour of the sky and the sea. It is always there, reliable and trustworthy. Blue is a very masculine colour communicating stability and strength. It is often used by finance and health brands because it indicates trust, loyalty, confidence, intelligence, logic, and success, as with Xero, Visa, PayPal.

Blue physically slows the human metabolism and produces tranquillity and calmness, and is often used for products and services related to reliability such as banking and communication. For example, ANZ, Facebook, Skype, Zoom.

Avoid using blue for food, hospitality, and cuisine brands because the colour blue can suppress the appetite.

Blue products and services are related to cleanliness (water purification filters, cleaning liquids, vodka), air and sky (airlines, airports, air conditioners), water and sea (sea voyages, mineral water).

Blue is more about intellect and sincerity compared to the spontaneous colours like yellow and red.

Blue is ideal for high-tech products and services because it conveys accuracy and reliability.

Dark blue is associated with depth, expertise, and steadiness. It is a preferred colour of corporate brands who want to communicate their stable and trustworthy leadership. Dark blue represents knowledge, mastery, integrity and authority.

Light blue is associated with health, healing, tranquillity, guidance, and trust.

White, Black, Silver

White is the colour of perfection, honesty, and simplicity. Pure as the snow. It opposes black and has a positive impact. White space is often used in brands to cleverly indicate a shape where there is none, creating an optical illusion.

White is used for low-weight, low-fat, and dairy products and services.

White also suggests simplicity and honesty in high-tech brands and charitable or health organisations.

World Wildlife Fund uses the negative space to create a panda.

The Playboy bunny logo uses white to appear wholesome.

Black is a very powerful colour, indicating fear, death, and evil as well as strength and seriousness.

It is a prestigious colour signifying authority, a black tie, black Mercedes, little black dress, or James Bond, 007.

Black can be used to give perspective and depth and is often used to make other brand colours stand out because it creates contrast, such as Adidas, Nike, Prada, Gillette, Sony.

Grey is a conservative colour, subdued, understated, controlled, mature and responsible.

Silver grey indicates elegance, glamour, and sophistication and is often used for brands perceived to be of high quality without being overly glitzy, like Apple, Jaguar, Swarovski.

It is an ideal secondary colour for brands who want to be seen as quality without overstating it.

Now that you know more about how colours make people feel, you can use them to communicate emotionally and have your ideal prospect react in certain ways when they interact with your brand.

But what about the other senses?

ALL THE SENSES

OUR SENSES PROVIDE information for our brain to create a perception. Is it light or dark, noisy or quiet, does something taste bitter or sweet, feel soft or hard?

Sound is one of our vital senses, one we often take for granted. It can be used to create a hidden message in your brand. Sound is vibration detected by tiny hairs and bones within our ears. Is your brand giving off good vibrations?

Sound feeds the brain information about our surroundings that can cause a physical reaction. A loud bang can make us jump, the sound of a tiny mosquito causes almost immediate panic, or we see the calming effect of a mother's lullaby that soothes her crying baby to sleep.

The amygdala in your brain uses sound to embed memory of an experience. Just consider the advertising jingles you still hum as an adult that you heard years ago as a kid listening to the radio or watching TV. How often do you have nostalgic memories when you hear a particular song from your youth?

Sound can also create an emotional state of desire as well as increasing the speed of decision-making. Consider the last time you were subjected to elevator music. Did it make you want to stay there or leave as fast as possible?

Funny how you instantly know when someone has an Apple Mac by the sound it makes when it turns on. Or that all too familiar 'dum-doom' when Netflix is loaded. Stephen Hawking had one of the most recognisable brand voices in the world and it was totally computer generated.

A brand's purpose is to create meaning and elicit an emotion, in order to make the client feel a specific way, assisting in purchase behaviour. Consider how it sounds inside a shopping centre verses a wellness spa or fitness centre. All of them play music in order to arouse certain emotions, feelings, and elicit actions from those who venture within.

Sound can be a vital element of branding, especially if you want it to be remembered and loved. Schweppes has taken their brand sound to a whole new level by coining and trademarking the phrase 'schweppervescence' to describe the sound their product makes when you break a cap on a bottle. Of course, every soda fizzes but schweppervescence is something else and something that brand owns. Schweppes has taken ownership of a sound and it has become more than just a noise, it's a state of being that only their brand can deliver.

A motor racing circuit needed to modernise its brand to become more attractive to a wider audience and they asked for our help. We listened to the sound of motorsport to understand what attracted people to the sport and what got them excited. We learn that each vehicle has a different sound and that the industry has unique and familiar voices, like the instantly recognisable commentary by the effervescent Murray Walker[47], who could make even the most boring of races sound exciting. He would scream when the red lights turned green at the start of a race, "Go, go, go!"

Murray once commented to a journalist that the sound of a Formula One car, "Goes right through you, disturbing the very rhythm of your heart." Suddenly we knew we had the essence for the new motor circuit brand for Manfeild. The sound of the brand became the main theme for the brand promise, the thing everyone can expect every time they visit the venue:

Feel Your Heart Racing

This is now the new tagline and it appears on all their merchandise, advertising, and billboards. It is also becomes part

---

[47] How Murray Walker became not just the Voice of F1, but a legend of the sport with his infectious personality, iconic enthusiasm and 'Murrayisms' as a commentator over 25 years —
https://www.skysports.com/f1/news/12433/12245153/murray-walker-remembering-the-voice-of-formula-1

of their new jingle: "Go, go, go, to Manfeild. Feel your heart racing." Before long the staff, race teams and visitors to the track are all singing along to the jingle or humming it to themselves.

An interesting side note is that the lyricist Charlie Sutherland, a renowned jingle creator who had been behind many of the big brand sounds, based the beat for the jingle off a track by a band called The Datsuns. Even the concept behind the music had something to do with cars.

Suddenly the Manfeild merchandise becomes as popular as Ford and Holden branded gear.

MANFEILD

Word-leading TV advertising producer Howard Grieve, who I had the pleasure of working with at Saatchi & Saatchi, once told me, "The way to know you have a jingle right is when you hear other people humming it." That's when a sound becomes an 'earworm,' something that sticks in your brain so that it can be instantly brought back into consciousness through unconscious acceptance of it as a tune worth remembering.

How can you use sound to define and promote your brand, deliver on its promise (by making people feel a certain way), or recall your brand subconsciously?

You can create a sound track or jingle or consider music on your website or in the background of your videos:

- How do you want to make people feel—calm, excited, happy, safe, hyped, relaxed, entertained, or alert?
- Does the sound you use do that?

144

YOUR BRAND TRUE NORTH

- When you create a video intro/outro, what sign-off sound can you use that communicates your brand?
- What sort of tune would you like to have your ideal customers humming?

Our brains use all senses to absorb and make sense of the world we live in so there is possibly nothing worse for a brand than the sound of silence.

When you think about how you want your brand to make people feel you can also consider the other senses and how they also create an instant message for your prospect's brain.

In terms of touch many 'purple' brands create a sense of smoothness, like Silk Cut cigarettes and Cadburys Chocolate. Others convey toughness, like rugged automotive brands Built Ford Tough, and the famous 'Levi's' with solid rivets and double stitching.

Our brain uses the sense of touch or feeling to understand our environment and recognise and form feelings about brands. Can you remember something that made your skin crawl, gave you goosebumps, or made the hairs on the back of your neck stand up? Touch creates body reactions, and those reactions can create powerful memories.

Can you choose the fabric or material for your product or packaging? The luxury lingerie brand Victoria's Secret extends their brand 'feel 'to their see-through shopping bags.

Apple invested heavily in the product packaging to draw out the feeling of 'un-boxing' your new device, delaying the purchase gratification by designing boxes that hold a release factor, slowing down the dopamine response to lengthen the enjoyment factor.

Taste can lead to individual preference—Do you love Pepsi or Coke? Chocolate brands spend billions trying to create a specific flavour. Wine makers take years to create a specific blend, often happening upon it by chance rather than design.

It's dark and dry in the cellar beneath the Abbey of Hautvillers as Dom Pierre Pérignon[xx] is turning the wine bottles carefully, handling each one like a prized chalice. The spiders have been busy and cobwebs are hanging over the racks like tiny vines making his hands sticky. *Must be all the rain we've been having this autumn*, he thinks, *that's what has driven these eight legged creatures inside.*

Suddenly the bottle in his hand almost explodes and the cork pops out with a loud bang startling him and making him jump backwards. Wine is sprayed all over him and as he licks his lips and attempts to wipe the wine off his face he notices something about the drink that causes him to stop and take a swig from the bottle. Bubbles! He excitedly calls to the other monks working in the cellar, "Come quickly, it's like drinking the stars!"

Champagne was discovered accidentally. There are actually a number of origin stories and the French and English have been fighting over it for years. Today the region of Champagne in France has declared that only wines from its vineyards can be called Champagne[xxi]. All others must be called sparkling wine.

All very well for food and beverage brands to have a taste specific to their brand, but if you are a leader or professional service provider, how can taste create a brand feeling? If you've had a poor experience you might say a brand 'left a bad taste in your mouth" You might respect a tasteful brand. Offering a sample of your product is to give a 'taster.'

What flavour is your brand? Sweet? Crunchy? Savoury? Strong? Fun? Light? Exciting? Fresh? You can indicate a brand feeling using descriptive words that also elicit a response from your prospect's brain without them actually having to eat or drink your brand.

And there is always a great opportunity to leave something if you provide a home service like pool servicing or house cleaning, or if give your clients gifts at Christmas time. You might make a gift of chocolate or wine based on how you want them to feel about your brand.

Smell is another sense that can elicit an emotional response. Perfumes are 100 percent invested in the sense of smell, often matching the fragrance personality to the celebrity who endorses it. Real estate agents suggest baking a cake or making coffee in your house before an open home to put people at ease and make them feel comfortable. Fast-food brands have long been accused of 'pumping 'aromatic smells outside of their stores to increase hunger pangs. Consider the 'new car 'smell of a showroom, or the fresh clean smell of a luxury hotel room, or the incense aroma of a day spa.

What's your brand's smell?

Can you include a scent inside the follow-up cards, mailers, or welcome packs you send to clients? Do you give candies or tea as gifts? What smell will match best with your brand personality and deliver on the promise?

The senses can create an instant emotion and you can use neurobranding to embed a memory about your brand experience deep into the subconscious brain of your ideal client. Even something as simple as choosing gloss or matt stock texture for your brochures and business cards makes customers feel a certain way about your brand.

Now that you know more about neurobranding and how the brain 'sees' brands, you can make better decisions to enable your brand to have more meaning and purpose in a highly competitive and overcrowded world. You now know how to create brand value using neurobranding science to make people feel a certain way about who you are or what your business does. Now you can create a stand-out brand that is going in the right direction.

You are ready to Find Your True North.

NORTH

"Efforts and courage are not enough
without purpose and direction."

~ John F. Kennedy

HOW FAR WILL YOU GO?

I WINCE SLIGHTLY at the pain in my back, but hold still, knowing any movement could be disastrous. This isn't the first time I've felt it, I had the same thing a few years before, but this time it's going to last longer and I'm getting my mindset ready to deal with this self-inflicted discomfort. The tattoo artist continues to work on the compass he is inking into my back and I stay still and as relaxed as I can. Thankfully, Link is a pro, with years of experience, and he is very proficient and fast. The result is perfect and I love it (you are welcome to see it on my social media pages) and it is my brand.

Would you go so far with your brand that you would tattoo it into your skin as a permanent marker of your True North? I met a salesman who was so passionate about the brand of beer, he had the logo on his arm and he could do a blind taste test and pick his beer. Then there is the gym owner with the NBA basketball logo tattooed on his calf. Many Australians have the Southern Cross constellation inked into their shoulders, in my home country of New Zealand they have ferns on their arms, and in the Pacific Islands tattoos tell entire stories.

The compass was not my first tattoo. I got the Libra birth sign inked after my 50th birthday. I wanted it for many years, knowing exactly what it looked like and where it was going to go. It even features in a book about tattoos I participated in to help raise funds for breast cancer research. But I knew when my Brand True North and The Brand Navigator came to fruition, that helping people with their brands is what I was born to do. I do it with ease and it fulfils and delights me. So I couldn't wait to get it permanently marked on my body. I know this will never change. My brand is part of my DNA and part of the way I conduct myself personally as well as in business. My brand gives me direction and helps me clarify my marketing messages, but also defines how I connect and communicate with the world and what I value most in life.

Do you feel like you are totally on your Brand True North? Are you so well aligned with your business brand, that you would get it tattooed into your skin? How far will you go to align with your brand? How much are you prepared to step into the brand so everyone recognises what you stand for and what you have positioned yourself as the leader for?

If you are not feeling 100 percent all-in, or if you feel disconnected from your brand, it's probably because there are mismatched values. You lack the purpose and reason to *be* your brand. It may be that you feel your talents and skills or Expert-Ease is not valued by the brand you work for, or if it's your own business, that your personal brand has no input or influence over the business brand. It may be that your guiding principles do not match those of the business or organisation you work with.

If there is a disconnect or feeling of being off the path of your brand direction, now is the time to consider why you are doing what you do.

NORTH is all about alignment. Knowing everything you stand for, knowing what drives you, and being on purpose with passion.

I am not suggesting for a minute that you go get inked (unless you really want to and you know what you want), I am asking the question to test your brand integrity. Integrity means a state of being whole, a complete entity. This is what branding is all about. You know by now that branding is far more than logos and colours, it is about creating meaning.

Here in NORTH you will define those things that hold up the integrity of your brand, that enable you to deliver the brand promise. It makes it easy for your team to understand why your brand and business does what it does.

NORTH is the final piece of your brand compass, and possibly the most important element that will form your personal brand and help you stand out as a leader.

WHY?

EVER ASKED YOURSELF, "Why am I here?" Of course some people have extraordinary natural talent, like the world-leading sports stars who were born to jump or run, kick or hit a ball better than others. They seem to have always known what they wanted to do and they, like Nike, "Just did it." Then there are the geeks, nerds, and tech-heads who type code better than they can spell and built their own tablet for their 10th birthday. Not only do they know their purpose, they can't quite figure out what the big deal is about finding it. Of course there are the entrepreneurs who, when they were knee-high to a grasshopper, were selling lemonade or trading baseball cards to their friends. They see the world in a completely different way than the rest of us and seem to always land on their feet.

But not everyone has such clarity. In fact we might even consider these 'super humans' freaks of nature. Most people either fall into their profession, taking an opportunity to earn an income and floating from one role to the next based on survival, rather than the desire to thrive. Or they have their genetic destiny chosen for them, brought into a family business or following their father's footsteps into a trade. As we get older the desperation to find your purpose gets more intense. There's the 'ticking clock' of reproductivity, the mid-life crisis of your 50's, and the desire to create a legacy before you leave this mortal coil.

Simon Sinek codified the why question with his TED Talk[48] about the 'Golden Circle,' highlighting that almost everyone can explain what they do and how they do it, but virtually no one shares *why* they do what they do. Knowing your WHY[49] explains how brands like Apple and personal brands like Martin Luther

---

[48] https://www.ted.com/

[49] The WHY is the purpose, cause or belief that drives every one of us. — https://simonsinek.com/find-your-why/

King stand out as different. They stand for something meaningful and they are well known for it.

The thing is, if you want to really have a massive impact, to inspire as many people as possible as a leader in your industry, you are going to have to find your purpose, the things that fire you up, create clarity, and give you the direction to promote and market your passion.

Probably the best piece of advice Simon Sinek gave in his TED Talk was, "People don't buy what you do, they buy why you do it." If you want to create a stand-out personal brand, lead in business, and attract a tribe of followers who become your raving-fan clients, you need to emotionally connect with a shared belief. If your brand and business is solely driven by money or fame it's far more difficult to have real emotional engagement with your audience or to naturally attract affiliates, clients, and partners. You have to fake it till you make it, and that's not really sustainable.

No matter how great your service is or how qualified you are to deliver it, if people can't connect with your purpose, they will never really trust you enough to believe in you or follow you.

PASSION & PURPOSE

IN THE BLAZING sun a young man stands in front of the Greek Acropolis, guidebook in hand, opened at the page depicting a beautiful frieze of the goddess Athena, the bringer of victory. He brings his hand up to his eyes to hide the glare of the sun, marvelling at the massive columns stretching heavenward above him, reaching into the clear blue sky. Standing there for a lengthy time, could be hours, every now and then, he shuffles his feet on the dusty clay ground, but he's not going anywhere. He is enraptured in the experience, drinking everything in.

This is one of the highlights he planned for on his impulsive adventure. That and a trip to Japan to talk to possible investors and manufacturers about his crazy sports shoe idea. As Phil Knight, founder of Nike, turns to leave, he notices a carving engraved into the temple's marble facade. Its Athena, also known as Nike, the Greek goddess of victory, and she is leaning down to adjust the strap of her shoe.

Now, suddenly everything about the Nike brand makes more sense doesn't it? Now you know *why* their brand talks about winning and victory at all costs. Now you know that being fast and winged like Nike gives meaning to the Swoosh logo.

When a brand is conceived from a place of purpose, with reason and meaning, the leader of the brand, and everyone who works within the business, knows it. You may not have known the Nike origins story until just now, but it doesn't matter, you already had an idea of what the brand was all about. That's because those at Nike did know the story. The leaders of the business lived it and their brand promise continues to be delivered around the world to this day. Everything they have done, all of their advertising, the way they promote and sell their products, the in-store experience, customer support, social media, sponsorships, celebrity endorsements, they all follow the brands one-word strategy: Victory.

And this all came from the founder's dream, passion, and purpose. His WHY.

That's what NORTH stands for, your passion and purpose. The thing that drives you and the legacy you want to create. The impact you seek and what you want to be well-known, well-paid, and wanted for.

Your True North is about more than being paid to do something. Yes profits are important, as are income and bonuses. We have to look after our family, pay the bills, and we all deserve nice things, holidays, and time with those we care about. But finding your True North is about knowing you are aligned with what you do and with the business brand.

Business owners, entrepreneurs, and leaders who know they are headed in the right direction, with total integrity and authenticity, lead teams of people and create a loyal client following. Not just because of who they are and their expertise, but because they confidently stand firm in the knowledge that they are on the right path.

It is far easier to follow a leader who consistently creates the same feeling within us, as someone we can trust, than it is to be convinced to follow someone we know is only in it for themselves. Winning sports teams have relentless leaders who set standards and consistently show up. Leading politicians have a way of encouraging and motivating people to believe in their policies.

154

Rock stars and celebrities ooze sex appeal or star values that their fans soak up and revel in.

Knowing what drives you, what your personal brand stands for, and then aligning yourself with the business brand, means not only do you stand out as the leader, you naturally attract the right business partners, investors, staff, and clients.

But how do really know what your WHY is?

In this chapter we will go deep into your values, beliefs, backstory, and personality. We will discover what drives you to be who you are and to do what you do. It will be a challenge and at times you may feel frustrated, or that you are going in circles, not able to see the wood for the trees. Don't panic, I'm here to help guide you. It's okay to get lost, as long as you have the tools to get back on your path.

This chapter is the culmination of your brand compass. You know who you help, what problems they have, and when and why they come to you. You know your Expert-Ease and how you have a unique way of resolving their problems. You know the outcome you deliver and why they should trust and value your leadership.

Now it's time to give people a reason to see you as their leader, to want to follow you, buy from you, and be led by you to the top of the mountain, the summit of success.

So why does the Nike story explain how to find your WHY so well? We all love stories, and that's because the brain is wired to make meaning of the things it is presented with. When our brain gets told a story, it releases feel-good oxytocin, enabling us to empathise with the story or the storyteller. So one of the best ways to explain your WHY, is to go back to the origin story. Just like the Marvel movies, they have expanded their universe by going back in time and giving fans what they want, a really good story that helps them make sense of the other movies.

And there is nothing like an *ah-ha* moment to cement a memory in our brains. It's how brands become really recognisable. The story gives the brand meaning and purpose, helping us connect and recall the brand. And that is especially valuable to businesses when it comes to persuading people to buy from us. It's especially vital if your product or service is technical or complicated, new or difficult to explain.

In 1996, three industry leaders, Intel, Ericsson, and Nokia, meet to discuss and strategize how to standardise short-range technology so connectivity and collaboration between different products and industries is possible. During this meeting, Jim Kardach of Intel suggests the code name Bluetooth as a temporary brand name while they are developing the tech. He has been reading about a Scandinavian King, Harald "Bluetooth" Gormsson, who was well-known for two things—uniting Denmark and Norway, bringing together a great nation with shared culture and values, and for having a dark blue/grey dead tooth. Harold united the land in the same way they want to unite the personal computing and cellular industries.

Later, when it comes time to select a serious name, the one they were going to use (PAN) was unavailable and a trademark can't be gained before the launch, So they stick with Bluetooth.

The Bluetooth logo is a combination of two ancient Scandinavian runes merging Harald Bluetooth's initials.

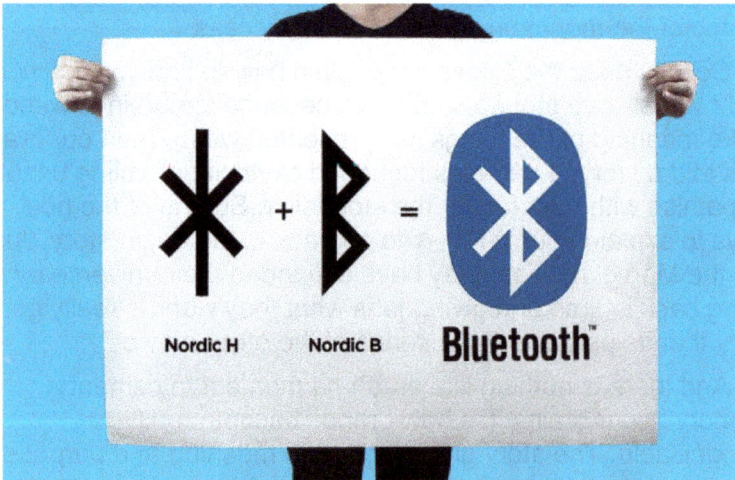

You probably use this technology to connect your devices, mouse, phone, laptop, wireless headset, and other devices and have seen the Bluetooth icon on them but until now had no idea what the brand name meant. You just know what it does for you. Bluetooth makes it easy to connect anything to anything.

Plug and Play

Until you learnt the brand story you probably thought Bluetooth was a technical term and now it is fast becoming a genericide for anything that seamlessly connects, regardless of if it uses Bluetooth or not. The stories behind brands give us connection to their values and beliefs. They make a brand more than just a company or a business trying to sell us their wares. They give us a sense of what the brand is all about.

If your ideal prospect shares the same values and wants the same outcome, they are naturally attracted by the brand story or feel good about connecting with you as the brand leader. Having a brand that tells a meaningful story helps you create marketing messages that reinforce what your brand does. If you tell that story well, your customers can become raving fans and storytellers.

You may now be wondering, *What is my story? How can I create something as meaningful as Nike or Bluetooth? What symbols can I use in my branding that tell a story?*

Just off the coast of Brisbane, Queensland, there is a tiny island renowned for its red sand. Coochiemudlo Island, accessible by ferry, is a major part of the local Quandamooka culture. During the hardest times when the English settlers forbade aboriginals from speaking their own language, they would go to the island to hunt and take the children into the bush, whispering the dialect to them to teach them the culture, scratching marks in the dirt to share their stories.

Many years later, once the land had been established with holiday homes, jetties, a few short roads, and very limited internet coverage, a section of land was purchased by the police department, and short-term accommodation was built for long-serving members' families to enjoy a breakaway. It was hardly ever used and as a result it was sold.

The new owners want a name for the retreat that reflects the history of the island and what it means to escape the everyday hustle and bustle and connect with each other and nature. They ask me to help them and I take a few weeks to speak to the local elders and research the words in the dictionaries of the Jandai language[50] at the Queensland University Library.

The ferry ride to the island is only 10 minutes but as we leave the mainland behind it feels like I am also leaving behind my cares and worries. I step off the boat and onto the wooden wharf, then onto the sand, and immediately my shoulders relax as I walk down the road into the shade of the trees.

At the retreat I meet the owner and present the concept behind the new brand, *Gindabara*—a word created from the Jandai language which means 'place of laughter.' The client loves it. The Gindabara brand identity uses the colours of the sea, sky, sand, and beach, and the logo is the symbol for a meeting place.

The tagline, 'Get Closer,' explains how close the island is to the mainland but also how you can get a closer connection to nature, each other, and yourself, when you stay there.

GINDABARA
GET CLOSER

---

[50] Jandai is the language of Quandamooka Country, Queensland. Spoken by members of the Nunukul, Goenpul and Ngugi[citation needed] people, now only few members still speak it. —https://en.wikipedia.org/wiki/Janday_language

If you are creating a new brand you can consider your brand origin story and look for symbols, shapes, and icons that will tell your brand story.

If you have an existing brand or are working under a corporate or franchise brand, make sure you find out the origin of the brand. Discover its purpose and meaning and why they chose the colours or icons or imagery. Understand the brand promise, purpose, and meaning, and see what aspects of the business' brand story align with your own personal brand values.

From a personal branding point of view, finding your WHY can be as simple as taking a look back in time to uncover your unique brand story. Then apply this to your bio, About page, social media, and other places, so those around you can better understand where you are coming from and why you behave, think, or feel a certain way about things.

Take the time to consider your journey:

- How did you get here?
- What drives you to keep doing what you do?
- What happened to you or to those around that made you so passionate about it?

Your True North gives you direction and purpose for all of your brand and marketing messages. It makes you stand out from the rest with an authentic reason and a depth of meaning that your ideal prospects, business partners, fellow board members, managers, or even future employers, can relate to. It can come from as far back as your childhood.

Di Krome softly emerges from her sleep, rubbing her eyes as her dad gently shakes her shoulder. "Come on," he says "time to go." It is still dark and cold but Di knows she needs to get up and help the family. She quickly dresses in her warmest clothes, slips on her comfy shoes, and rushes out the door with her brothers. They scramble into the milk van and Dad starts it up, headlights blazing into the darkness.

Di hates these early mornings and getting up while everyone else is still sleeping. Her brothers jostle about, annoying each other and joking around. She looks out the window, silent and grumpy. She can't wait until the round is over and they can go home. That's the place she really loves. Sitting at the kitchen table counting the money and sliding the coins down the change-counter slots. She loves the smell and feel of the money and the sound of the coins clinking together. Why can't she just do this bit?

Not surprisingly Di does well at school and she becomes an accountant. While working at a large firm she experiences firsthand what badly run workplaces are like and decides she's had enough—*There must be more to life than money*. She is challenged with health issues and starts to put wellness first. Then she opens her own consulting business, advising small businesses in the wellness industry.

Di and I work together to reposition her brand to move away from the "equilibrium" of the accounting world to fire up businesses to not only be profitable, but to look after their most valuable asset, their people and their wellbeing.

Di is now a Workplace Wellness Consultant and her brand is called Wildfire because she reignites people's passion for business.

Finding Your True North is about finding where your natural talents and learnt skills intersect with your life purpose. When you combine these you find direction for your brand, both in business and in life. After all, branding and positioning yourself as the leader is about being fulfilled and actively living your life as a whole person, using your whole *self* to be rewarded, happy, productive, and influential. Finding your True North is about discovering how you can combine *everything* about you into one powerful brand that impacts the world.

I'm sitting on the hard plastic seat of the rickety old school bus, chugging along the winding road on the 30-minute journey from the safe haven of Hunua to the South Auckland township of Papakura. We turn in the gates to the high school and kids pile off the bus and lope[51] off into the main hall. Coming from a tiny country school I'm bewildered at the size of the place and all the different people surrounding me. It's all so new and confusing. *Where do I go? Which is my home room? What class am I meant to be in next?*

Even though I feel lost at the start and stay well inside my shy shell, I love to be creative and lose myself in the things I enjoy, immersing myself in art classes, playing sports, trying fun science experiments, attempting typing (which is hopeless as my dyslexia really shows up and slows me down), and I discover the language and culture of Japan from our wonderful teacher, Mr. Wong. He is a Buddha of a man in stature and personality. Much as I like his teaching style, I really love the curving script of Hiragana[52] and the symbolism of the language. Mr. Wong also shares insight into the culture and values of the Japanese people. He tells us they have a saying for finding the source of value in your life and how to live a blissful life, doing what you love, and giving you reason to wake up in the morning.

---

[51] Lope: an easy usually bounding gait capable of being sustained for a long time —https://www.merriam-webster.com/dictionary/lope

[52] Hiragana is a Japanese syllabary, part of the Japanese writing system, along with katakana as well as kanji. It is a phonetic lettering system. The word hiragana literally means "flowing" or "simple" kana ("simple" originally as contrasted with kanji). —https://en.wikipedia.org/wiki/Hiragana

They call it *ikigai*. Roughly translated into English it means "finding your purpose," and it is the foundation of finding the True North for your brand. Although ikigai is not tied to your financial status, the business world has morphed ikigai into not only doing what you love but also getting paid well to do it. Having a blissful life is a nice idea but you still have to pay for your mortgage, car, food, kids' school fees, and a nice vacation every year. Until the world adopts a minimal guaranteed income for everyone (and that's a bit of a pipe dream) we can't be solely spiritual beings, focused exclusively on simply doing what we love. We need to be practical as well.

Even if you are a digital nomad with low overhead and no ties, you still need an income to live. I have met such people in Thailand and Vietnam, competent, skilled professionals who simply cut back more and more into their lifestyle and daily costs in order to survive by earning just enough to live. The less they earn the more frugally they live. To me, that is not living a blissful or fulfilled life.

The real secret to achieving a blissful life doing what you love and being paid for it is to ensure you are doing something that people want and you are doing it with passion and purpose. Finding your Brand True North is all about being fulfilled by more than earning an income. I'm sure you have had jobs that paid well but didn't fulfil you. Chasing the money can make seeking a blissful life quite stressful because it limits your joy.

Instead of enjoying using your natural talents and aligning your skills with your purpose and feeling valued, needed, and feeling that you have made an impact, you sabotage your success by worrying about pleasing others. If you allow money to dictate your value it becomes easy to get caught up in imposter syndrome, worrying that someone will find out you are a fraud an having a lack mentality that belittles your worth.

If money is the reason for your purpose and passion it will hold back your true potential. Try to consider what you earn as an outcome from doing what you love. Get your brand positioned right and you can earn whatever you want, simply by being a leader in your field. Know it will take time and while you build your brand you may have to do work that doesn't bring you joy but eventually, if you have a strong enough purpose, you will get there.

There is no magic spell or silver bullet. This entire book outlines the process you are undertaking to find Your Brand True North, and it will take a few years for you to build a successful, recognised and respected brand. You may well have a few moments when you question the path you are on and after using this book you may decide you need to go in a new direction or find another path to the one you are on.

The purpose of this book is to guide you to choose which mountain you want to climb, then set your sights on the summit. As you progress through this final point of your brand compass you may even get the clarity to know you are in exactly the right place and have been all along, and it will confirm you are already on your way to having a stand-out brand, that your natural talents align with what you do, how you do it, and why you are so passionate about it.

Time to consider what you were born to do:

- Where do your natural gifts, expertise, and experience meet with your goals in life?

- What has life taught you that is now your approach, value, or methodology?

- What really annoys you about the industry you work in that you'd like to change?

- What are you so in love with doing that you can imagine doing it forever?

Michael lives in his family home in the U.K., spending most of his spare time after school and in the holidays upstairs in his bedroom making models. Aeroplanes, cars, trains, he loves them all, but mostly he likes making the ones that are superbly designed with fiddly little parts and tricky stickers. He spends hours at his desk, working away under the glow of the lamp, carefully opening each kit and checking that all the parts are there before starting to form the pieces together. He takes his time to make sure everything is exactly right. It takes days and even weeks but he doesn't rush it, painstakingly painting each model with exactly the right colours, attaching the decals in precisely the right places.

At last he has finished and he sits back and stretches his neck and shoulders and looks down to admire his handy work.

When Michael grows up he becomes a *bespoke jeweller*[53]. You'll remember him from the Burgundy Bespoke Jewellery brand story you read in $OUTH.

Michael's superpower is detail. He's been doing it all his life.

- What did you love doing as a kid that you still love now?
- What stories from childhood have formed the person you have become?
- What challenges did you overcome?
- What made you who you are?

Being paid well for doing what you love, enjoying every minute of it, and making sure that is something others want from you, is where you find your *ikigai*. Knowing what it is you want to be well-known, well-paid and wanted for, is your personal brand. This has got to be a dream for most humans, earning nicely doing what they love rather than exchanging their time for money, or worse, doing something they really dislike until they can afford to live their dream.

You obviously love what you do as a business owner, manager, or entrepreneur, and you deserve the respect that earns you the ability to charge what you want.

There are a number of exercises you can go through to help you find the purpose behind your brand and help you become

---

[53] Bespoke jewelry is one trend that just keeps getting bigger. You might be hearing the phrase "bespoke jewelry" getting thrown around a lot these days, but what exactly does it mean? Bespoke jewelry refers to jewelry that is made especially for a client or customer. —https://cadcamnyc.com/blogs/our-blog/bespoke-jewelry-what-does-it-mean

recognised as the go-to leader with a reputation as being the best.

The exercises in the following chapters come with a warning: After considering these questions you may want to take a break from chasing the dream you always *thought* you had and instead take some time to figure out what it is you love doing. When you have more purpose and direction, you may very well choose a new dream.

Find somewhere quiet and take your time to answer these questions. Make notes or record your thoughts. If you feel you are going in circles or get stuck, allow the questions to sit for a while without an answer. If needed, dwell on them. Go for a walk or find something to take your mind off the topic and then the answers may find you.

You will be taken back in time to find the defining moments that created your WHY. Be prepared to revisit the past. Some memories may be painful, or fun. Let them be what they are, knowing everything in your brand matters and everything you are counts. There are no right or wrong answers and no such things as strengths and weaknesses. You are what you are. Don't try to change what makes you, you.

Embrace your reason for being here and use it as the foundation for your True North.

PERSONAL BRAND

IT'S LATE ON April 6th, 2007. Arianna is still at her desk answering emails and taking calls. Her fledgling business is only two years old and she is putting in enormous hours to sustain its growth. It's exhausting but she knows it's worth it, if only everything she is working on started to come off, to roll and build on its own without needing her to push it along. Just one more email, one last call, and she can rest. She chuckles to herself. *Rest? What's that?* Didn't she just tell someone today that rest was for the weak and she could sleep when she was dead?

The world blacks out and Arianna suddenly finds herself on the floor. "Mummy, what's wrong?" Her daughter is standing over her and with tears in her eyes as she struggles to shake Arianna awake.

"Ooh, my head." Arianna touches her cheek. Her hand comes away sticky with her own blood. *What on earth has happened?* Slowly, she pushes herself up until she is balanced, half lying, half sitting on the ground. She looks down seeing a pool of blood on the floor and she hugs her daughter to comfort her that Mummy is okay. She wonders, *How long was I out?*

Her doctors diagnose her with exhaustion and Arianna Huffington's life changes. She starts to take better care of herself and put her personal wellbeing first. As a result, her business and her own personal brand thrive. She continues to launch and grow the news aggregator and blog, and authors a range of books, many about life balance, wellness, sustainability, and ironically, the importance of sleep. She eventually steps down from her CEO role of the *Huffington Post* when it is well established and successful and launches her new brand, Thrive Global[54].

---

[54] Thrive Global is an American company that provides behavior change technology. It was founded by Arianna Huffington in August 2016. The company is based in New York City. —https://en.wikipedia.org/wiki/Thrive_Global

Of course, it shouldn't take a dramatic event to help you find your WHY, but sometimes that can be the motivator. You may be able to pinpoint a time in your life when you got that clarity.

Not all of us have a moment like Arianna that pivots our story or kicks off a chain reaction in our life that can become our WHY. We may certainly know people who we feel have had far worse experiences than our own that shaped their life purpose. Most of us think we have very dull, boring, or tedious lives and may not have had a real 'lightbulb' moment that could create an engaging personal brand story, or so we think.

It wasn't easy for me to find my brand story until I sat down with a journalist, someone who gets paid to seek out and tell stories, and she pointed out how my dyslexia had become my superpower.

Everyone has a superpower. Some of us have more than one.

What's yours?

- What do you feel most proud of?
- At what moment(s) have you been at your happiest, fist-pumping the air, or doing a happy dance to celebrate?
- Remember your Expert-Ease? The exercise with the fingers on your hand?
- Consider the times in your life when this was most apparent. When you were simply doing what you love?
- If you are still unsure you can ask your clients what is it that they love about working with you.
- Ask your associates, friends and family when it is that they see you the happiest and what they think your natural abilities are.
- Then look into your past. What did you do as a child that you absolutely loved, like Michael the jeweller with his models, or Dianne, counting the milk money?

- What activity from your childhood have you brought forward with you to where you are now?

Consider all of your special gifts and talents you were provided in your DNA, the things handed down to you from your parents. My dad was an engineering draughtsman and my mother was a florist. I often joke that as a child I used lots of vivid tones to colour, but I always stayed inside the lines, thanks to my genetics.

What you were naturally born to do can have an extraordinary bearing on your personal brand and the type of career or business you get into. It may even guide you to start up something entirely new. However, being totally unique isn't always a benefit to your brand or business. If you want to be the in-demand brand that people value and pay for, being new or totally uncommon can be more difficult than you think.

I've managed to find a car parking space and grab my things before slamming the car door shut and racing inside. I've driven across town to be here, fitting in this meeting on a hectic day in the city. I just hope the man I'm meeting is on time. I've never met him before and I don't want to be late to my next appointment. He had contacted me at the last minute to see if we could have a coffee and discuss how I might be able to help him get his brand off the ground. I was wary and for good reason.

I see a man sitting on his own and wave. *Yes it's him.* He rises from his seat and shakes my hand. I order a tea and take out my notepad as we make small talk. Eventually, he begins to tell me how excited he is about his business and that he has big plans for it. He then says something that gets every red flag in my mind waving crazily.

With a bright smile and a glint in his eye, he tilts his head to one side, dropping his jaw and looking up at me like he is sharing the world's biggest secret. In hushed tones he whispers to me, "No one else is doing this!"

Inside I crumble, *Oh no, not another one!*

I cannot tell you how many times I have met entrepreneurs who are excited about a new idea they have created, telling me with gusto that the best thing about it is that it is totally new and utterly unique. It's not the innovation or invention that scares me, it's the feeling they have decided that for some reason being an exception is an 'opportunity' without understanding how consumers behave and buy.

Like most I have met, he wants me to sign an NDA before he will even tell me what it is all about. His fear and mindset of scarcity is palpable. He is so afraid someone will steal his money-making idea and profit from it, just like Edison stole Tesla's ideas.

Yes new ideas can be an opportunity and most entrepreneurs get excited about these things, but there is one major drawback of being first to market. No one knows about the problem you solve and no one realises they need your product or service to solve it. If no one is providing the solution you have developed, it's possibly because no one wants it. If you haven't already had people putting a down payment on your idea, you need to prove you actually have a *minimal viable product or proposition* (MVP) before you build a brand.

Almost everything we need on Earth has been designed, developed, or created. We've come a long way from fire and the wheel. Some of the best brands today are improvements on something that already existed. Uber modernised the taxi industry and Airbnb disrupted the accommodation sector in the same way the iPhone crushed the camera market and killed off Kodak.

We can always develop and improve things that exist. There are many technologies that have replaced services that had been around for decades and no longer exist. Anyone want to fax something or record a DVD?

Some improvements are not always better for the consumer, either. Remember when you could actually get service at a service station or how people were employed at supermarket checkouts? Those have been 'improved' over the years but at the expense of customer service.

Innovations and improvements to something that already exist are much easier for consumers to adopt than totally new

169

ideas and concepts that no one can see a need for. It is not good enough to develop something awesome, there has to be a demand for it.

Remember you can change attitudes but it's hard to get people to change their behaviour. There are lots of apps that get developed and never work out because even if they are clever, they aren't really needed. There are also many successful brands that started because the entrepreneur and leader behind the brand had a problem they needed to solve for themselves.

Janine is having a total blast in the U.S.A., loving every minute of the trip. She cannot believe how into health and wellness everyone seems to be. There are so many smoothies and juices to try. Back home in Australia where fast food is the norm she wishes there were the same products available for her and her family. She has an idea.

She is experimenting with combinations of fruit and flavours in the kitchen of her home in Melbourne, trying to avoid anything with additives or nasties. With zero experience in wellness she meets with nutritionists and dieticians to ask for their insight, finessing the juice recipes until she has what she thinks are the right blends.

Along with her husband Jeff she creates a retail model but can't get funding. No bank seems interested in a business concept whose product is liquid. But for three years she stays true to her goal even though she is earning nothing from her idea, and eventually she opens three stores, two of them on the same day. They then take the plunge and sign an agreement to open 28 stores in Westfield shopping centres[55] and in 18 months they become one of the country's top juice-selling brands.

---

[55] Westfield Group was an Australian shopping centre company that existed from 1960 to 2014, when it split into two independent companies: Scentre Group, which now owns and operates the Australian and New Zealand Westfield shopping centre portfolio; and Westfield Corporation, which continued to own and operate the American and European center portfolio. — https://en.wikipedia.org/wiki/Westfield_Group

Boost Juice[xxii] is now valued at $350 million thanks to Janine's original purpose and passion for health, fun, and loving life.

Solving a problem is vital if you want to grow a brand and be profitable. People have to want to buy it. There are many brands that are well-known but not profitable (WeWork[56] and Uber[57] to name a few) mostly because they get caught in the 'freemium' trap. People want what they have but aren't so needy that they want to pay for it.

Melanie is tired, it's been an incredibly long day and she leans back in her chair to stretch her neck. She's been looking at a computer screen for hours but after a full on day of lectures and brain-numbing study she cannot get a particular issue out of her mind. As a communication and commerce student she has been using her design skills to help fellow students with their assignments, but it is taking up so much of her time and is so tedious. *There has to be a better way.*

Not only are there so many different platforms and processes to achieve something as simple as producing a poster or flyer, many of them don't work well together, all of them need to have a steep learning curve, and most are too expensive for what they do. Students are always trying to find their way around tech issues and avoid costly subscriptions or programs, but it just takes way too long to do it the way it's being done. Melanie has no idea how to solve the problem, but she can tell someone has to, and expects someone will do it soon. So she picks one aspect of the problem, school yearbooks, pays freelancers to create a program, and launches Fusion Books[58].

---

[56] https://qz.com/2011851/will-wework-ever-make-money/

[57] https://www.forbes.com/sites/lensherman/2017/12/14/why-cant-uber-make-money/?sh=63e340b410ec

[58] Fusion Books was founded by Perkins and Obrecht in 2007. Fusion Books allowed students to design their own school yearbooks by using a simple drag-and-drop tool equipped with a library of design templates that could be populated with photos, illustrations, and fonts. — https://en.wikipedia.org/wiki/Melanie_Perkins

Through early success solving problems, building an easy-to-use platform, and some gutsy moves to secure funding, the business rebrands as Canva and becomes a $2 billion success. Canva eats into the market share of Adobe and Photoshop because it is so much easier to use and you can get started for free. They have millions of free accounts but have become profitable by making a paid membership valuable to users who really want even more ease and convenience. Tools such as clearcutting at the click of a button, team sharing, and extensive image and video libraries make the Canva[xxiii] experience so convenient for users prepared to pay. And pay they do. And they keep paying, happily renewing their subscriptions each year because now they can't live without it.

People are prepared to pay for perceived value as long as they trust the brand is looking after them and making life easy. If your brand can create long-term value you will have a large and loyal client base.

Some brands offer better technology to attempt to differentiate on value and they still lose to cheaper competitors.

The Sony corporation is at war. They propose a single format for recording video so the industry will have a standardised product and competition can be based on quality. But JVC has other ideas, introducing a different format despite Sony's pleadings. Sony appeals to the Japanese Ministry of Trade and Industry and it seems this is a brand battle, to be fought in the courts to choose which technology will win.

Betamax[59] is respected by the movie industry as higher-grade but there is a massive problem for users. The Betamax tapes can only record 60 minutes. The machines used to record and play the tapes are also more expensive. Most movies are at least 120

---

[59] Betamax (also known as Beta, as in its logo) is a consumer-level analog recording and cassette format of magnetic tape for video, commonly known as a video cassette recorder. It was developed by Sony and was released in Japan on May 10, 1975, followed by the US in November of the same year. Betamax is widely considered to be obsolete, having lost the videotape format war which saw its closest rival, VHS, dominate most markets. — https://en.wikipedia.org/wiki/Betamax

minutes long, meaning a movie watcher would have to change tapes halfway through a movie. JVC achieves a 120-minute capability, then RCA manages 240 minutes. Together they combine forces and launch a new technology, VHS, officially 'Video Home System.'

Consumers choose convenience over quality and the battle is over.

Now of course, even that technology is dead, but the point remains. You can never consider that just because something you have or do is better that it will become the leading brand. It is all about demand and which brand helps the most people achieve their goal.

When it comes to your Expert-Ease and leadership:

- How can you and your business or brand provide an awesome outcome that is better than your competitors?

- How do you improve something or make someone's life better, job easier, daily tasks more convenient?

- How do you give them something more than what they would expect?

- How many people want what you do?

- Do you have a waiting list or are you spending most of your time trying to convince people they need you and your services or products?

If there is no demand you have to educate people that there is even a problem. If there is an easier way to accomplish something, even if it is poorer quality, chances are humans will choose the easy way out. Consider more than what people need. Everyone needs a dentist once a year, but do we want to go see them?

A need becomes a want because we have some sort of problem which has become a nagging pain that now has to be acted upon. People then search for help, Googling the pain points and asking for referrals.

- So what pain does your natural talent, the thing you love doing, solve for others?
- Why does it matter so much that you solve it for them?
- What solution does your brand provide that you feel totally committed to and you know delivers a better outcome for those you sell to or provide for?
- Not just what you think, but what you *know* to be true?
- How valuable is your brand and its solution to them and why does it mean so much to you?
- What value does your brand provide that your clients cannot live without?

Remember to go to the core of the problem to truly understand what is causing it, getting clear on the pain and feelings they are experiencing. Is it stress, lack of time, loss of connection, feeling overwhelmed or out of control, being sick and tired (or tired of being sick), feeling useless, ugly, unfit or unhealthy, lonely, or unfulfilled? Perhaps they want more, need guidance, know they can't do it alone, want a leader, need to feel important or needed?

People want to know, like, and trust the person they are working with or being led by, but when it comes down to choosing someone, they buy your confidence and your passion and care less about how you do what you do. If it comes down to price they will always come back to the basic question, "Do I really need this?" and if your brand hasn't connected with their values they may use cost as the deciding factor to in fact do nothing. It's definitely an option to most humans. Apathy is always competing with you.

If you are unsure about the problem you solve, go back to WEST and get clear on your ideal client. Make them real and step into their shoes, consider their pain and what they need and how you can turn a need into a want by painting a picture of the outcome.

Not sure about why they should choose you? Go back to EAST and consider how your Expert-Ease can deliver what they want, and now, why they would choose you, your brand, business, or leadership to get them where they want to be.

Still unsure you are worthy of calling yourself a leader? Unsure about your value and what outcome you deliver? Review SOUTH and paint the picture again of the transformation you and you alone can deliver.

When it comes to providing a WHY it's about having common values and beliefs and having a brand that gets to people right where they are, with a promise that makes sense to them.

- Does the clean pool equate to enjoying a weekend at home with the family? In your marketing message you can share how much you love doing that with your family and how much more time you get to do that by having someone else do it.

- Does the correct life insurance policy equate to a stress-free lifestyle knowing your family is safe? Share how they can now sleep easy at night, knowing their family is protected.

- Does having a driving instructor your kid really connects with equate to keeping a teenager from the accident and emergency department or worse? Share how relieved you are that your kid's got the best training from the driving school so you know they are safe.

- Does having a project manager who delivers more than they were asked, under budget, and on time equate to less stress, happier shareholders, and increased chances to pick up even better contacts? Share how a project you managed did exactly this and how proud you were to be able to deliver it.

It's easy to create meaningful marketing messages when you know your brand connects and engages with your audience. When you put yourself in the shoes of your ideal client, what would you want as the outcome? How would it make you feel? What is it about how your brand provides the solution to the problem that would make you choose you?

Review your marketing messages, your bio, C.V., or About page, and count how many times you share something personal about why you do what you do. Do you talk about the problem and why you are so passionate about solving it, or is your content all about how you do things?

Remember many things today are replaceable, by apps or robots or AI, and services such as bookkeeping, accounting, travel assistance, and even legal services have been totally disrupted. But personal skills, natural, creative talents, and the feeling that someone actually cares about the outcome can never be replicated.

World-renowned business consultant John Demartini[60] says, "Until you value yourself, you can't expect anyone else to do so." Value *who you are* and everything that makes you, you, knowing the reason why you are so passionate about what you do makes your brand promise an absolute treasure.

Your WHY is a vital ingredient to your perceived brand value. Make sure you are not hiding it away.

If you hesitate to get too real or if you think your brand story shares too much of your personal journey, you may be tempted to copy someone else's story or appropriate something that isn't yours. Don't. It's not worth it. This is not the time to make things up or try to be the next Oprah, Vaynerchuk, Musk, or Branson.

Your entrepreneurial brain has the most amazing way of seeing opportunity and creating new ideas, but if you let it run amok[61] and don't have a clear sense of direction, your own brain can distract and divert you into desperation territory.

---

[60] Dr. John Demartini is a polymath and a world-renowned human behavior expert. His work has been described by students as the "most comprehensive body of work", "an extensive library of wisdom". Dr. John Demartini's mission and vision is to share knowledge and wisdom that empowers you to become a master of your own life and destiny. He's an internationally published author, a global educator and the founder of the Demartini Method, a revolutionary tool in modern psychology. —https://drdemartini.com/

[61] Amok: to be out of control and act in a wild or dangerous manner — https://dictionary.cambridge.org/us/dictionary/english/amok

We live in the age of authenticity and the brain of your ideal prospect is on high alert to false promises and will smell a rat from a mile away. Copying others, making up your backstory, or adding embellishments will erode your credibility, and more than anything, you will know that you are not being true to your brand.

A confused mind will never buy and if you struggle to keep track of a fabricated brand story, it not only creates even more confusion and overwhelm for you, it does the same for your audience.

Use the following exercises to help you discover your real Brand True North and develop your unique brand story so you can use your purpose and direction to stand out from the crowd and give meaning to your marketing messages.

Use the tips to help you through. Take a deep breath and don't be impatient. Give yourself time to consider, review, and work on your WHY.

It might take you some time, but it's worth it.

FIND YOUR WAY

THE NORTH QUESTIONS will be challenging. You may have never been asked them before. Here are some tips to help navigate your way through them:

Take Time Out

Many people feel pressured to 'find their WHY' and begin pushing or directing your thinking, rather than letting your purpose find you. Stressing about having to decide your life purpose is like looking down the barrel of redundancy, divorce, or financial ruin. Trying to figure out your WHY with a gun to your head is not pleasant.

When you relax it's amazing what happens to your brain and how clarity of thought can be created. Taking a break, exercising, or simply taking a shower can lead to the most interesting thoughts and clarity of direction. Greek mathematician and inventor Archimedes had his eureka moment in the bath and so could you.

During meditation beta waves[62] in our brain decrease, enabling it to process much less information. The frontal lobe which is used for making decisions goes AWOL and the parietal lobe and thalamus shut down the senses, losing you in space and time. This is where magic can happen. A bit of quiet time to reflect and allow your emotions to take over your rational brain can be all you need.

There is no right or wrong way to meditate, just let your brain relax and allow clarity to begin. Make note of how you feel, as the thoughts enter your brain, about your single-minded purpose. Even if you think it's woo-woo, give it a try!

---

[62] A step down are beta waves, which is what most of us experience most of the time in our always-on society. —https://www.wellandgood.com/brainwaves-biohack-sleep-health-focus/

Having a Brand True North compass doesn't mean you will never get lost. As an expert and business leader I frequently feel overwhelmed and have to go back and review what I am doing, making sure I am staying on track. My entrepreneurial brain still diverts and distracts me. The difference is with a solid purpose and clear direction you never stay lost for long, you just get temporarily misplaced.

There is a really great way to make sure you stay on track when you go through the questions to define your NORTH.

Ask

I know for some of you this won't come naturally. Either you feel asking for help is a sign of weakness or you don't believe someone else might know you better than you do. I'm certainly not the only woman who has endured the frustrating experience of being in a car with a man who is lost but won't stop to ask directions. The reason it frustrates me—a solid Eagle in terms of Personal Communication Style (PCS)—is that I feel *not* stopping and asking for help is such a waste of time.

It angers me when my husband gets in the car and without knowing where we are going, starts the ignition and heads off. Then the closer we get to the destination the more stressed I get. I would rather take a few minutes to find out where I'm headed so we don't waste any time going the wrong way.

If you get lost as you progress through the questions that follow and become tangled up in your own thoughts or feel you are going in circles, I suggest you ask those around you for the answers.

- The question, "What was it I did for you," is ideal to ask your existing clients if you provide a service.

- If you are their leader, ask them, "How would you describe me to others?"

- With friends and family, those who have known you personally for a while, ask them, "What are the things you recall most about me when you think of me?"
- Ask them, "How do I make you feel?" and . . .
- "What words would you use to describe my greatest strengths?"

Listen carefully to the words they use to describe your unique abilities and skills. Then peruse the feedback and you will see similar-meaning words and phrases that help you define your why. Your brand personality and the brand culture you develop that stems from your personal brand can all be derived from the emotion and the memory you create in the minds of others.

Let's find Your Brand True North by getting clear on your brands Single-Minded Purpose.

SINGLE-MINDED PURPOSE

GUS VAN DE ROER is the last person in the now-darkened office. With the desk lamp illuminating his shadow on the wall, he looks up from his work and notices everyone else has gone home. *Perfect*, he thinks as he rises from his chair and makes his way around the large oak desk. *Time to see what ideas are there for me!* He ventures out into the modern open-plan office in the boutique design agency and reaches the module of his creative team. He bends down to inspect the waste basket, pulling out three or four crumpled balls of A3-size paper that have been tossed away. On the papers he sees drawings, sketches, and doodles the art director has been working on that were dismissed as not good enough.

Gus stands up and takes the sheets back to his office, smoothing out the creases, and taking a good look at them before filing them away in the draw under his desk. He knows that although the ideas might not be ideal for the current client they are working on, they might be perfect for the next campaign. He trusts his team is talented and, thanks to his Dutch heritage, he doesn't want to waste one good idea.

Being creative is a gift and everyone reading this book has it. Yes, that includes you!

If you have started your own business or have stepped up as a franchise owner or business leader you have done something superhuman with your brain. Inside your brain there is a safety device called the *amygdala*[63] and it stops you from making potentially poor decisions.

---

[63] Amygdala is the integrative center for emotions, emotional behavior, and motivation. If the brain is turned upside down the end of the structure continuous with the hippocampus is called the uncus. If you peel away uncus you will expose the amygdala which abuts the anterior of the hippocampus. — https://nba.uth.tmc.edu/neuroscience/m/s4/chapter06.html

Notice I said potentially? This is because the amygdala is capable of making up scenarios about failure, risk, danger, and precariousness. After all, FEAR stands for 'False Expectations Appearing Real.' When you decided to go into business for yourself or set yourself apart as a leader in your industry, your fear centre was screaming at you to stop, telling you all sorts of doom and gloom stories to try to keep you 'safe.' Can you recall the alarming messages you began to think about at the time?

What you did when your amygdala set off its defences was something extraordinary. You overpowered the fear centre inside your own brain. You said to yourself, "It's okay, I know there are risks, but I'm going to do it anyway."

That's the superhuman power entrepreneurs have and it is brilliant but deadly. Your superhuman brain is more capable of being creative because it has less fear. The trouble is that with every superpower there is always the kryptonite, and in your case, you have something called 'bright shiny objectitis,' the ability to see far more potential opportunities than the normal brain does, and ignore the fear signals your brain is trying to tell you.

You can probably recall times when you jumped in at every opportunity or headed off in multiple directions. With an entrepreneurial brain you see opportunities everywhere, which is great because you can be incredibly creative, adaptable, and innovative. But it could also be killing your business, because when you see all the opportunities and possibilities you begin to suffer from something called FOMO—the Fear Of Missing Out. You don't want to 'miss out' on all those potential clients out there and you want to be 'everything to everyone.'

But, like Gus Van de Roer, who collected ideas for later use, you can harness your superpower and get creative, but also consider if it is right for your brand. Then, if it's not the right idea, time, or place, you can file them away for later rather than impulsively acting on them. The only way to do this is to decide what your niche is and what your brand stands for, what it does and doesn't do. *The brand becomes a litmus test for your entrepreneurial brain.*

I know that if you are a service provider or consultant it can be difficult for you to even consider narrowing down your "inch-wide, mile-deep' niche because you probably believe your service can help just about anyone.

FOMO is one of the main reasons most service providers struggle to find and communicate their point of difference to stand out from their competitors, and why they look like everyone else and are unable to charge a premium.

Think about it for a moment:

- Do you have a specific target audience and a finely-tuned strategy?
- Do you know exactly when you are 'swimming in your lane'?
- Can you easily explain your specific area of expertise?

When you lack direction and look like every other service provider or consultant in your industry, there is no point of difference and no compelling reason why someone should choose you. Going after *everyone* is virtually impossible, especially on a small marketing budget, and being scattered and inconsistent with your messaging is detrimental to your brand. It devalues your brand's trust currency.

If you really want to become a sought-after leader in your field with ideal prospects falling over themselves to work with you, and raving-fan clients referring you and doing your marketing for you, you are going to have to focus on being an expert provider of a particular type of service for a certain type of person.

If you want a stand-out brand, it is vitally important to become known as a specialist.

I hurt my knee while sailing (or could it have been at the gym?). I can't recall how I did it but it is not getting better. Every time I put weight on it, it hurts, and it is starting to ache at night. Eventually I decide I need to see a doctor. I know there is a clinic at the local shopping centre because I've seen the big sign out front. I call to get an appointment and they say they can get me in tomorrow.

I arrive and sit in the waiting room a while until I eventually get to see the doctor who asks me a load of questions. She gets me to flex my knee and pokes and prods it to see what hurts. She suggests I need to see a specialist as it may be a tendon issue and she knows exactly who I should go to for treatment. She signs the referral letter and sends off the email, giving me a prescription for pain medication. I limp back out to the reception area. I pay $80 and head home and take the first of many anti-inflammatory pills because I know it's going to take a few weeks to hear back from the specialist.

A month later I get my appointment notice and a month after that I go to the knee doctor. I meet him in the specialist clinic and we chat briefly. Even though I have no idea how I caused the injury, he knows exactly what the problem is and suggests a course of treatments including physiotherapy, ultrasound, and acupuncture. I get more referrals for more specialists and leave after paying the bill, which is much more than the general practitioner's cost.

At least I know I am in good hands and I can trust that a solution is near. I can almost feel my knee getting better already.

Which would you rather be? The low-paid, overworked generalist who has to advertise their services to help everyone and is constantly looking for new clients, charging the minimum amount the industry allows, or the well-paid, exclusive, and widely-recommended specialist who is well-known for a particular set of skills, naturally attracting clients from generalists, surrounding himself with other specialists and charging whatever he wants?

Specialists get paid more than generalists because they are sought-after, referred-to, and respected. Your goal should be to be the specialist, so you can focus on doing just what you are really good at, and being valued and respected for that. The way to become this go-to leader is to find your niche. This means a couple of vital things will happen to your brand and your business:

- You know exactly who your ideal target audience is, making it easier to connect and capture their attention because you know how to get their brains interested in your services or products and you can increase conversion rates,

- You can use your natural talents, skills, and expertise to cater to their specific needs to become known for what you do best with recognition as a leader, standing out from the competition,

- Your clients become your raving fans and you get loads more referrals from them and other specialists because people are comfortable to trust and recommend you,

- You can dictate where you work and when your skills, services, or products are available, creating scarcity and demand for your brand,

- You can charge more for your expertise and be the leader in your industry—well-known, well-paid and wanted!

I know you may struggle with marketing and may have already lost hundreds if not thousands of dollars on wasting time on promotional activity that didn't work (WOFTAM), and you may be concerned that you really don't have the knowledge or the time for choosing a niche. You may be worried that you have invested so much already into your business or brand, and if you choose a niche or to niche further, you will miss out on opportunities. You may be confused by social media and overwhelmed by all the terminology, or perplexed by your peers and all the marketing 'gurus' telling you, "You know what you should do. . ."

But if your marketing activity right now is knee-jerk reaction and guesswork, it is costly and ineffective at best, and soul-destroying at worst. If you are truly honest with yourself, you know what you are doing is unsustainable and something has to change.

By finding Your Brand True North and following the process in this book, you can develop your own unique niche and use that as a platform to build *anything*.

The process for NORTH starts in one place, *you*. If you are unsure what your one thing (specialty) is, it's worth understanding the quote by Plato, 'Know thyself.' To know thyself is an ancient Greek phrase inscribed at the Temple of Apollo at Delphi, and has had a variety of meanings attributed to it in literature. The best translation I believe is that in order to find peace and become who we were meant to be in life, we need to have a very clear and strong understanding of who we are.

Jeff Bezos, CEO of Amazon, said, "Personal branding is what people say about you once you have left the room." Yes, it is about reputation, but I'd like to go a bit further than that. True North is like ikigai, the merging of your ideal clients—the people you most want to help or work with—alongside your Expert-Ease—the things you do with ease that others find difficult—and the reason, purpose, and passion behind why you do it.

Finding Your Brand True NORTH is all about defining your Single-Minded Purpose (SMP).

Over the following pages you will be guided through a series of five key questions. These can be used to develop the niche for your personal brand or your business brand. They can also be used in a team environment to help you create a brand promise or to develop your brand mission and values statements. You can use these questions to develop your brand culture and even provide a foundation for your deliverables and terms and conditions.

Take your time with these. Don't rush the answers. Consider the questions deeply and consider if your answers are just the standard responses, or if they are really deeply meaningful.

SMP #1

"A problem is a chance for you to do your best."

~ Duke Ellington

When is Your Brand at its Best?

Anita scrolls through the social media pages on her phone getting more and more worried about the increase in desperate pleas and posts she sees from menopausal women. She notices a growing number of adverts for invasive treatments and costly procedures that she knows are really not necessary, and she believes most of the advice being shared is misleading and dangerous.

And now that young start-up newbie with next-to-no experience has opened a yoga studio just down the road. She is really worried her potential clients might be swayed by cliched memes and Instagram reels.

If only she could help more women get their energy, vitality, and love of life back naturally without all the motions and potions on offer. That's all she wants to do, and she's had so much success she knows she is good at it.

Her business is called 'Anita's Yoga,' but she offers so much more than that. She needs to find a way to position herself and her brand so she can stand out from the competition. That is the only way she can help more people, using her unique approach.

Anita asks for my help and we discuss the outcome she wants to deliver, how her approach transforms people's lives, and the impact she wants to have on the world. She tells me most come to her sick and tired of feeling sick and tired. They are overweight and over it. Their thyroid packed up and left, their energy is non-existent, and they feel life is just so unfair.

Menopause happens right when the kids have become more independent and women are just getting their lives back. Then suddenly they are hot and sweaty insomniacs with get-up-and-go that got-up-and-went. What they want is to find their mojo. To feel alive, zesty, full of vitality, and vivaciousness. They want their life back and they are looking for a way to spark their energy levels.

Vurv* is born, and Anita begins to position herself as the go-to for menopause, with a tagline that shares the brand promise, 'Jumpstart Your Life!'

You probably already know when you are at your best and this should help you define when your business is at its best. It's not about what time of year you love most or if you are a morning of afternoon person (although these are interesting personal traits). Being at your best is when you feel you are operating at 100 percent, giving it everything and delivering on your promises. When you are at your best as a leader you are full of confidence, acting purposefully, using all our expertise and experience.

Being at your best is when:

- You feel you are in 'flow' and everything comes easy to you,
- You love the activity so much it doesn't feel like work and nothing is a chore,
- You feel you are utilising all of your natural talents and skills and being of value,
- You are working in total harmony with others and in the environment,
- You are focused and engaged without feeling like it takes effort or learning,
- You feel totally at ease, being truly who you are and doing what you love.
- What were you doing that, when you looked up from it, you noticed that time had flown by?
- When were you most happy, feeling rewarded and having a life that mattered?
- What do you do that you feel is your life purpose?
- What are your best traits, skills, talents, or natural abilities?
- What did you get the best marks for at school?
- What do you avoid doing so that you can get back to what you enjoy most?
- What do the testimonials or reviews you get say most about you?

It is not always possible to create a brand and earn a living going fishing, playing sports, or sitting on the couch binge-watching Netflix. That is not the purpose of these questions. You need to frame them in terms of your profession, your leadership, the business you have created, or the venture or project you head up.

Knowing what you do best is the key to personal branding, defining your leadership by knowing your niche and staying in your lane. Your brand is at its best when you are doing what you love. Your business is at its best when it's delivering that to clients.

Go through and answer those questions above and think back to a time when you were most proud of yourself. What were you doing? What did you achieve? How did you do it?

You might want to make a list of all the things you do in your day and highlight the ones you love to do, or you can even rate them on a scale of 1-10.

Review what your day includes and notice how much of it is spent on doing things you are not the best at.

In order to stand out with a strong personal and business brand you need to be totally consistent, otherwise your brand promise will not match the brand experience. If you are not delivering on your promises perhaps it's time to divest yourself of the things that are not enabling you to be your best. Delegate or start saying no.

The best way to know if you and your business are operating at their best is to ask yourself, "Are we overdelivering on our promises, or overpromising and underdelivering?"

It's important that you focus on the things you do well because it will be far easier to maintain your brand when you and the business are doing the things you love. It will show up in the customer reviews and testimonials you receive.

- List all the things your business does well and how it delivers on its promises.

- Consider all the small things that automatically happen that you don't tend to mention but are vital to operations.

- Think of how your business does things differently to others and how that makes life easier for the team and your clients.

- Think about the natural abilities, soft skills, and personal traits of your team. How do they work together to provide something exceptional that no other business brand offers?

- Consider what your brand promises to deliver and check that you are achieving that or if you are falling short.

This is all part of finding your niche and focusing on the hidden treasure beneath the surface of your personal brand and the business brand.

An amazing woman who really struggled to find her niche once asked for my advice. She was an office manager and incredibly proficient and capable. She had been in high-powered corporate life and enjoyed it but was not happy being bossed about and undervalued by her managers, who were mostly men. She wanted to start her own consulting business but worried about overcoming her fear of working with men. The goal was to help business owners sort out their business and be more efficient. She had already identified that her target client was more likely to be male than female.

We overcame this fear by focusing on the things she did really well, things she could be 100 percent confident about. Her organisational skills and the ability to see issues before they became problems were key. She also knew she had a great skill for negotiating with staff, ensuring businesses could make changes and know staff would implement them. She found a gap in the market for her natural skills and talents and she cemented herself there, gaining confidence to overcome her doubts. She has gone on to found not one but three businesses managing both men and women with ease.

"When you're in a market of professionals where your brand has to be you, it really helps to identify your key strengths and then market yourself in a way that makes you stand out."

- Rachel Berry, The Barista Academy

So now answer this question for both your personal and your business brand:

"My brand is at its best when: _____."

SMP #2

"Be careful not to compromise what you want most,
for what you want now."

~ Zig Ziglar

What Will Your Brand Never Do?

Nolene sighs as she rounds the corner of the high street[64], shaking her head in disbelief. There is yet another audiologist clinic with a bright banner on the windows, and right in front of her on the pavement is a sign promoting *free* hearing tests. *Free*, she thinks, looking down at the pavement and wishing there was something she could do. Her hands have curled into fists, she is so angry. *How can they do this to people?* she rages to herself. *It is such a rip-off!*

It's mid 1980s and Nolene is a qualified audiologist with an entire career built on personal integrity. She has a dream of helping people hear properly and is really being tested by this latest trend in offering sub-standard hearing tests to lure people into clinics.

She is incredibly grateful when Audiology Australia later tells hearing centres that they cannot use these freebies as 'loss-leaders.' Sadly, she knows, however, far too many people now have hearing devices they paid thousands for that will probably be sitting in bedside drawers and bathroom cabinets not being used, all because they weren't tested properly.

At least the misleading promise of a free hearing test is gone, or so Nolene thinks.

Fast forward to the 2000s and hearing centres now offer 'free' hearing tests practically everywhere. Nolene has opened a new clinic and she flatly refuses to do this. When we meet to discuss her brand positioning we decide there is an opportunity to 'lift the lid' on the industry and make sure people know what they are really getting (or not getting) from a free test.

She starts promoting the fact that her hearing tests are affordable, that you will get a full and proper test, and that you can even bring your own hearing aids with you to check they are

---

[64] High street: a street where the most important stores and businesses in a town are —https://dictionary.cambridge.org/us/dictionary/english/high-street

correct and get them fitted properly. She appears in magazines with her story and within weeks she has lines of people wanting her services, all because she won't do what the industry is doing.

"When you start in business you can get lost very quickly. It's hard to see the best way to go. You need a clear target to aim for rather than being everything to everyone."
~ Nolene Nielson, Hearing Care Professionals

Compromise is part of doing business. When I worked in advertising agency production management there was always a place for compromise between the client brief, the creative, and what could actually be achieved in the timeframe and budget.

On one instance a direct marketing campaign idea was developed that required a tiny piece of meteorite to be fixed to about 10,000 items. This was before the internet and you couldn't simply Google it. We got on the phone and after many hours of enquiries we eventually found some of the elusive space rock, but it would cost thousands of dollars and was way above the budget available. The compromise was to spray paint rocks to make them look like bits of meteor.

Compromise is even more evident in the corporate world where all the different departments and stakeholders have to be allowed for and everyone needs to be kept happy.

At AXA I headed up a project to redevelop the website to function better for clients. The first thing I did was take a walk up to the customer service team on the next floor and ask them, "What is the first thing you need to know in order to help a client?" Turns out the *knowing their location* was the most vital step. Only then could the customer service team find an agent in their area and put them in touch.

It was obvious the website needed to start with a map of the country with an interactive link to click on your region to find an advisor. This part was easy as we had all the advisers details

YOUR BRAND TRUE NORTH

already on file. The difficult part was when we tested the site and had so many calls from agents wanting their profile to be at the number one position. This was impossible to do, not everyone could be first on the list, so the compromise was to make them appear in alphabetical order by surname.

When it comes to branding there are some things you will never compromise on and these are likely to be values you developed long ago that steer you throughout life. This is what forms the basis of your brand promise and makes you stand out as different from competitors.

A builder once shared some brilliant insight with me. He said there were three things you can have: cheap, fast, or good, but you can never have all three.

- It will be built fast and cheap but not be very good quality,

- Or it will be good and fast but it's going to cost more,

- Or cheap and good but it will take more time.

In business if you drop your standards your brand value will also drop. Thinking, *She'll be alright*, or, *It will do*, are the words of the average. If you want to be compared to others and painted with the same brush as them, compromising on what you deliver is the way to get there.

Think about the core beliefs you have about what you deliver as a service or product guarantee:

- What will you never quit on?

- What would you fight to the death for?

- What will you never do?

- What will your business brand never deliver?

- What is the industry doing that you dislike and won't do?

- Where do you draw the line when it comes to compromise? (In the immortal words of Meat Loaf, "I'll do anything but I won't do that.")

- What sets you apart from the competition because of what you won't or don't do?

This is about finding your niche by choosing not only what you do best but also choosing what you say no to—the hearing specialist who doesn't give away free hearing tests, even though the entire industry uses that as a marketing ploy, the back-pain specialist who never uses the words, 'pain management program' because unlike all the physiotherapists and chiropractors offering ongoing treatments, his focus is on *removing* the pain.

Make another list, this time all the things that you and your brand will never do.

SMP #3

"Set your goals high, and don't stop 'till you get there."

~ Bo Jackson

Where Will Your Brand Be In Three Years' Time?

Aaron sits on the windowsill of the small timber house perched on the water's edge in the bay opposite the city. It's late afternoon and the summer sun is warm on his face, the beer in his hand is cold. He glances over the carpark at the disused army barracks where his printing business, Twins Digital, is housed. Noticing there are cars outside the shed he can tell that his brother and team are still working. He shakes his head and thinks, *Man we are putting in some crazy hours.*

He wipes the sweat from his brow and takes another look at the invoices and paperwork on the bench next to him. The business is growing fast, almost too fast. He's going to have to make some firm decisions. He takes in a deep breath and sighs. As the sun begins to dip beneath the hill he wonders, *How are we going to do this? We can't keep bankrolling this thing without some sort of idea to drive the business, and a focus for where to invest in.*

Dealing with crazy deadlines each day is bad enough, but the demand on his time to organise machinery, equipment, and supplies is driving him mad. If only they could stop coming up with more new ways to do things and settle on what they want the business to be. Then he could plan ahead more and strategically grow the business.

After meeting with us and getting clear on his brand personality, target avatar, and niche, he decides what he wants to do. Everyone agrees and we set out his goals and where they want the brand to be in three years' time. They set a BHAG (Big Hairy Audacious Goal) and write their mission statement on the wall: To be the biggest large-format printer in the country.

He makes a list of all the ideal clients they need to go after to make their dream business come to life. He creates a plan to manage the investment in machinery, costs, and marketing that needs to be done in order to deliver on the brand promise.

Three years later Aaron contacts us. They are celebrating picking up every single client they had listed. They have changed the brand to 'SuperColour,' and have taken over the top position, putting some competitors out of business. Their single-minded focus on where they wanted to be has become a reality.

"The biggest thing you did for us was getting us started down the path that we're on now— the vision, culture, and focus for us and our brand."
~ Aaron Waddington, Director, SuperColour Printing

As a business leader or entrepreneur you can be tempted to jump from one bright idea to the next which can create distrust because of your inconsistency. You know as an entrepreneur you have a superhuman brain and you have overpowered the fear centre or amygdala so you are wide open to opportunity. You also know 'bright-shiny-objectitis' can lead you astray and spread you thin if you try to climb too many mountains or go off in all directions. We all know how exhausting it is to walk down lots of different paths that lead us nowhere, and having to retrace our steps or start all over again.

Having a three-year goal will help keep you focused and on track and stop you from getting lost in your own overwhelming world. Three years ahead is not too far to create lofty or vague goals such as having a bigger factory, more staff, better paying clients. Three years is also not too short that your goals seem totally unachievable or that when these things don't happen you make up stories to overcome the disappointment.

As a leader you probably worry that if you niche too much or set too specific a goal you will miss out on opportunities or limit your success. You could also be wondering what happens if something changes and your goal becomes irrelevant or impossible.

The secret to having a brand goal and strategy that withstand the test of time or economic changes is to focus on what impact your brand will make on others' lives, not just your own.

Pete stands back in his white chef's uniform, surveying the scene. With his arms folded across his ample chest he wonders if they have done enough. To the untrained eyes this looks like chaos, but in the pandemonium of the noisy restaurant kitchen Pete can see the carefully planned and developed systems and processes he and the team have worked so hard on, making sure there is consistency in quality for every dish that goes out.

Smash! A plate falls to the ground and smashes into smithereens. Everyone jumps and Pete rolls his eyes. *Not now,* he thinks. *This is the last thing we need in the middle of a frantic dinner service.*

Today could be the day they will know if they have a coveted Michelin star and everyone is on edge. Little does Pete know Michelin didn't start out with the intention of grading and rating chefs and their restaurants. The goal he so covets isn't even their main business. Michelin is the second largest supplier of tyres in the world. So what do they have to do with restaurants?

Way back in the late 1800s, two brothers started a tyre manufacturing business which eventually developed and trademarked the radial tyre technology used today. In the early 1900s they created touring guides and maps to encourage drivers to get out more and sample the local areas. Their goal was to have more vehicles on the road, driving more miles, so that more tyres were used.

By 1926, the Michelin star-rating system was created and it quickly became a sought-after guide for savvy consumers who wanted to make sure the places they visit are worth the drive.

So the goal of selling more tyres became a goal for worthy chefs to strive for. It seems an unlikely pairing of goals, yet it works. The Michelin brand and its logo (which was recently rated the greatest logo of the 20th century[xxiv]) have withstood the challenge of time, surviving through world wars, economic booms and collapses, and a pandemic.

Three-year goals help you stay focused on what your brand needs to become. The goals enable you to have confident and purpose-driven marketing so you can avoid having too many messages that make your brand come across scattered and desperate. Three year goals are better than having no goals. Being directionless leads to marketing that confuses your audience and makes them start to doubt your intentions.

For example, have you attended a networking event and someone handed you a business card that had one business on one side and another on the back? How did that make you feel about them? You probably thought they were hedging their bets and I bet you felt pretty unsure of their intentions or capabilities. Confucius said, "You can't chase two rabbits," and he was right.

When you set a goal to be specific about what you want to achieve and where you want to go it becomes very easy to 'litmus test' every opportunity to decide if it's a path worth going down or if it's just a distraction.

When business leaders create strategic or business plans however, they often use broad, sweeping, and non-specific terms, or they have personal goals such as having a nice house or an expensive car. We can fall into the trap of making up goals just to suit ourselves instead of being specific and focused on what we want to achieve as a leader or business owner.

It's like going to a medium to have your future read in the cards and getting a vague and ambiguous response then weaving your own meaning into what they predict to satisfy your own outcomes.

The brain wants things simple and it wants precise instructions, so your goals need to be specific. Decide what you want for your business and where you want your brand to be in three years' time, or you will continue to waft about, reactively dealing with what life throws at you.

Without specific goals and ideas about where you are going and how you will get there you will continue to suffer from FOMO (Fear Of Missing Out), simply go after everyone you think could be a potential client, and end up offering services or products you aren't really aligned with or good at.

Without a plan, the bright-shiny-objectitis you have will continue to highlight all sorts of opportunities and possibilities. You will weave off course, losing your focus, and travel down many dead end roads, costing you time and money and getting you nowhere near your goals.

If you want to attract perfect clients and have them recommend your products or services to others, or to attract ideal candidates to join your team, you need to be focused and consistent.

If you want to become the credible leader in your industry you need to become like one of the well-known brands we have mentioned in this book, instantly recognisable and on a mission to fulfil a purpose.

Having specific, defined goals will help you start to focus and stay on course. If you worry again that you are defining a niche that is too narrow, just remember you have an entrepreneurial brain which is capable of creating opportunities from nothing, and as long as it is on-brand you will be working towards your goal.

When you are on your True North you will know instinctively when an idea is perfect and if it is going to help take you closer to your goal or if it is just a distraction, taking you away from where you want your brand to be.

So let's now set some goals for your brand. For example:

What will your business look like?

- How large will it be?
- How many staff?
- How many locations?
- What sort of products or services will you sell?
- Where will you get them from or how will you make them?
- How will they be delivered?

- What machinery, resources, or skills do you need to get there?
- What clients will you have?
- How will you be attracting them?
- Who will be referring people to you?

What will you be like?

- What will you be doing with your time?
- How many hours will you work?
- What roles will you have and what will others do for you?
- What qualifications or skills do you need to accomplish that?
- What activities will you be doing to grow your brand?
- Will you have books, podcasts, blogs, or other tangible assets you create?
- What people do you associate with?
- What groups, memberships, or associations do you belong to?
- What do people call you #1 for? What are you known for?

How will you be recognised?

- What awards will you or your business win?
- What media will you appear in?
- What podcasts or TV/YouTube shows will you be interviewed on?
- What market share will your brand have?
- What level of brand awareness will it have?
- How will your brand be rated compared to competitors?

- Who will be endorsing the brand, promoting, or recommending it?

By being as specific as possible about where you want your brand to be in three years you can even create a business plan that runs alongside your brand strategy.

Get clear, set some goals, and outline your destination.

Where will your brand be in three years' time?

SMP #4

"Be sure you put your feet in the right place,
then stand firm."

~ Abraham Lincoln

The Three Things Your Brand Stands For

Paul sits on the beach watching surfers enjoying the morning waves. He feels sick. He's in so much pain he can hardly move. Even walking to the beach these days is torture. There is no way he can get back on a board in this state. He feels weighed down, his pain tying him to the beach like invisible chains. He is over all the pills, the constant pain management plans, the treatments, and endless specialists who can't help him. Nothing seems to work.

He looks down at the book he has been loaned by a friend, yet another person trying to help him. It was a kind gesture but he is dubious. *What on Earth could be in this book about breathing, posture, and something called 'Alexander Technique' that can help when all the other treatments haven't?*

He reaches down, wincing as he moves and takes another longing look at the surf. He sighs and opens the book to the first page and starts reading.

Twelve months later Paul is pain-free and surfing again. He cannot believe the transformation he has achieved by using simple practices actors use to maintain posture and breath. He has immersed himself in the technique and has become a practitioner, and is starting to help others remove pain from their lives, but he is still struggling to explain what he does.

His mission is to bring this pragmatic science of self-management and natural coordination to the masses, but every time he tries to explain it people think he's a chiropractor or physiotherapist. He needs to find a way to stand out and instantly demonstrate what makes his brand different.

We work together on a brand strategy and Amoči is born—a Sanskrit word that means, 'liberty and release from bonds.' It communicates how people, chained down with pain like he was, can be set free of it.

He begins to call himself a *back pain removalist* and clearly states he will never offer a pain management plan because he knows that's what the industry offers and it doesn't work. He offers freedom from pain.

Paul's brand stands for liberty, relief, and practical knowledge. The first time he uses his new core message at an event, people are falling over themselves to get his business card.

What are the three things your brand stands for?

The strongest and most stable shape in nature is a triangle. The construction industry has known this for years. With three sides, a triangle remains strong and rigid even when the maximum pressure is applied to it. In the same way that a triangle can support immense pressure, it is important to have three values that form your brand foundation, the three pillars that hold everything up. A three-sided object such as a three-legged stool is also very economical. There is no need for a fourth leg, three will do fine to give your brand all the strength it needs to carry the business.

You don't need to have a long list of values, just three simple, solid, foundational values you always deliver on.

Interestingly, the shape of a triangle cannot change unless all three angles change which means that if one side is to alter it effects all three sides. In the same way the three things our brand stands for are reliant on each other. Take one away and your brand promise cannot be delivered.

Paul could deliver freedom from pain, liberty from those bonds, and he could share practical knowledge, but unless it actually gives you relief, it doesn't work. You wouldn't keep putting in the effort without results.

So let's now concentrate on discovering the three most important factors your brand stand for, that, if you took one away, your entire purpose would falter and fail, the three most important things that keep you and your business strong, stable, and able to withstand plenty of pressure.

Many brands use the word integrity in their mission statement. Integrity is often misinterpreted as simple honesty. It's much more than that. Integrity means, 'in entirety, whole, sound, unified, undivided.' The three things you stand for should be so integral to you that they remain deeply imbedded in your subconscious, defining who you are and how you behave. So you can't have one of the three things your brand stands for as integrity, because having all three is what gives your brand integrity.

The three things you stand for are so vital they are etched into your personal and business brand. They are so meaningful to you, you could tattoo them on your body.

My brand stands for: Having a clear sense of purpose, stepping outside your comfort zone, and taking action. Having a compass tattooed into my back is a no-brainer when you know what my brand stands for.

You might start by considering a list of important factors, deliverables, or values your brand has and working backwards to find the top three most important, the three that must remain stable for your brand to exist, and for your brand promise to be delivered. What three values does your brand have that rely on each other in order for you to fulfil your purpose? What three beliefs define your purpose and will never change, always remaining the same throughout your entire life as a leader, business owner, or human being?

These three things don't need to be singular words, they can be phrases. For example:

- Always tell the truth.
- Stay focused.
- Constantly delivering on time.
- Genuinely caring about others.
- Push through the comfort zone.
- Continual innovation.
- Technology tested in the field.
- Safety first.

Consider the unique approach you have to what you do and the things you hold most sacred when you deliver outcomes to others. Start making a list and test them out to find your three value statements.

The way to test them is to check if they operate separately from each other. Often you can have values that are too close. For example:

- Honesty and truth,
- Safety and caution,
- Health and wellness.

When you know you have three totally separate values you can see if it's possible to deliver on your brand promise if you take one away.

For example, with Your Brand True North, there is no way I can give the best brand advice if I require focus on the purpose and stepping outside of your comfort zone without taking action. My brand also fails if I suggest taking action, outside of your comfort zone, without having purpose. And if you have purpose and take action but stay well inside your comfort zone, your brand will never reach the heights of its full potential.

Time to answer the question:

"The 3 things my brand stands for are: _____."

SMP #5

"At the end of the day, you can't control the results,
you can only control your effort level and your focus."

~ Ben Zobrist

Your Brand One Word

Steve is tearing his hair out, storming around the boardroom, glass walls shaking with his rage, and everyone in the office has started staring. The engineers gathered together in the room are looking at each other worried all their hard work is going to be destroyed.

"There must be a way!" Steve shouts as the team huddles around the sleek boardroom table. "We have to make it smaller or it will be totally pointless even launching the damn thing!"

An engineer hesitantly speaks up in defence of the others, "Steve, there's just no way we can fit everything in if we make it smaller. He then utters the words no one uses inside these walls: "It can't be done."

Steve looks him dead in the eye for a few seconds and then glances out through the glass at the office where everyone has stopped what they are doing to watch the spectacle. Quickly, as if caught like naughty school children, they all rush about to get back to their work, trying to avoid his gaze.

He notices the fish tank in the reception area with tropical colours of the fish flashing around the crystal-clear blue water. It's meant to be soothing and a way to calm guests visiting the high-tech office space that houses hundreds of staff and millions of dollars in technology hidden behind the design lab doors.

He storms out of the boardroom and strides across the office, followed anxiously by the engineering team who have worked so hard on yet another 'never been done before' project. He stops in front of the reception area, holding the device by the corner. He neatly drops it into the tank[xxv]. As it sinks to the bottom, a stream of tiny bubbles escape into the water. "See," he says. "There is space in there! Get back to the drawing board and make it smaller." The iPad goes on to become one of the top-selling devices of all time.

Apple stands for innovation and thanks to the passion, drive, and purpose of its co-founder Steve Jobs, everyone knows it.

213

Even after Steve leaves this mortal coil, his brand legacy of innovation lives on.

Think different.

Chaleo Yoovidhya is standing in the corner of the dark, noisy studio where Muay Thai[65] fighters are sweating it out in the ring. Bystanders are shouting and cheering on their favourites, tourists are sitting on the benches trying to work out what's going on. He finishes setting up his stall with bottles of Krating Daeng ready to sell. He's been selling the drinks to truck drivers, labourers, and students to help them with energy, concentration, and productivity. If he can keep getting to these fighting events being seen and noticed by sports stars, he's hopeful his invention will make him a fortune.

It's unseasonably hot as Dietrich wipes perspiration from his forehead with an already soaking wet handkerchief. He feels the sweat dripping down his back and his headache is not going away. He landed in Thailand only a few hours ago and he's worried the jet lag is going to ruin his trip. Looking up from the dirty streetscape in the bustling market, he sees his friend at the entrance to the Muay Thai studio where they agreed to meet, and

---

[65] Muay Thai, which translates to "Thai Boxing", is the national sport of Thailand. Muay Thai is a stand-up striking sport, with two competitors in the ring throwing punches, elbows, knees and kicks at each other. — https://yokkao.com/pages/what-is-muay-thai

hopes it is air conditioned inside. Unfortunately for Dietrich, it's not.

After the first fight he decides to go to the bathroom to freshen up and see if that helps rid him of this brain fog. He pushes past the crowd wildly cheering on the fight, noticing a drinks stand with its bright banners and bottles. He stops on the way back to his seat and takes a look, picking up a bottle, leaning in and cupping a hand to his ear to hear what Chaleo is saying.

Through the noise and Thai-English accent he picks up the word 'energy' and reaches into his pocket to hand over the foreign notes to buy a bottle. Taking the top off immediately he sips the contents as he continues back to the benches where his friend is waiting.

Within minutes of downing the drink, Dietrich feels alive, his head is clearing, and he is much more like his usual self again. He excuses himself from his friend and goes back to have a discussion with the seller about what is in this miracle drink, only to find the drink's inventor is a pharmacist. He learns the drink's name and roughly translates as *red gaur*, meaning red bull.

Red Bull[xxvi] is known for energy, sponsoring all sorts of high-octane events and stunts that amaze the world and help the brand live up to its promise of 'giving you wings.' It now sponsors extreme sports events and is mixed with vodka in bars around the world.

RED BULL GIVES YOU WIIINGS.

215

Sven can't believe it! He's gone and done it! His hands tremble and he leans against the machine set into the concrete of the vast factory in southern Sweden. The late-spring sunlight streams in through the windows, dappling his overalls and his head drops to his chest in relief as he realises for certain that his invention works. How many times they tried and failed yet now the double-row spherical bearing was not only holding up to the challenge, it was working! It was rolling!

He patents his idea and five years later purchases the trademark for Volvo[xxvii], meaning "I roll" in Latin, preparing to sell millions of bearings to the American market. But the world war has started and his plans are scuppered by the need for bearings in heavy vehicles and trucks. Sven starts up the SKF manufacturing company to make the most of the opportunity to help the war effort. He puts his bearings away in a drawer and forgets about them for twelve long years.

Assar and Gustav have been working together in the factory for a long time but today they meet at a seafood restaurant in Stockholm to discuss their innovative ideas. Assar has been scrimping and saving every part of his commission while working as managing director at SKF, but he needs Gustav's engineering skills to make the plan work. Together at the table over the steaming hot meal they lean in close to discuss how on Earth they are going to make 10 prototype vehicles and then convince SKF to get behind the project.

On a cold August day in 1926, SKF sign the contract with Assar and Gustav, purchasing the project for the first Volvo cars to go into production. Excitedly, Assar and Gustav shake hands, smiling from ear to ear with satisfaction.

As production begins, they make one proviso, that the guiding principle behind everything made at Volvo is and must remain *safety*. The Volvo brand is centred on safety. Their logo contains the symbol for iron, reflecting the strength of the Swedish steel industry and communicating properties of safety, quality, and durability.

Every stand-out brand has *one word* at its core. Everything they do stems from that word. They don't have to use that word as their brand name or even in their tagline. They use other words that mean the same thing and are memorable and catchy.

A brand's One Word creates a focal point for the brand purpose. It gives the marketing meaning and creates a platform to develop the brand personality and culture.

- Apple = Innovation = Think Different
- Red Bull = Energy = Gives You Wings
- Volvo = Safety = For Life
- Nike = Victory = Just Do It
- BMW = Success = Ultimate Driving Machine

So many marketing people, leaders, and business owners try to dream up snappy taglines or mission statements to define their purposes. These often contain flowery, elaborate, and jargonistic language. They look great on the wall of the office, in a corporate brochure, or on the Home page of your website but, instead of helping others to clearly understand you and your personal brand, these statements are too wordy and meaningless. They cloud the vision and confuse anyone who interacts with your brand.

- Having *one* word that your brand owns as a focal point is a powerful way to develop a brand identity and create a brand culture for others to follow.
- Focusing on one word that defines you can be difficult but when you do get it, it's absolute gold!
- Having one word that you can focus your brand on makes it simple and easy to remain focused and ensure that everything you say and do is on purpose.

Using the thesaurus can help you find words that have double meaning or other words that sound different but mean the same thing.

My One Word, not surprising, is *Direction*. Everything I do with my brand has purpose and meaning. It is thought out, coordinated. It helps guide others and creates clarity to align everything to be focused on the brand message.

Take some time now to consider what your One Word is. Don't rush it. Be prepared to think back to how you got started in business. Consider your original story:

- What you loved doing as a kid,
- How you want your brand to make people feel,
- The outcome you deliver,
- Your brand promise,
- Your values, purpose, and passion.

For your business brand, consider what one word best sums up the total parts of the operation:

- Service,
- Technology,
- People.

Then go deeper:

- Trust,
- Tested,
- Patience.

Keep going until you have a short list of possible words to use. They may even be similar sounding words, or different words that almost mean the same thing. Look at history, Sanskrit, Latin, Greek mythology. Google is your friend when it comes to etymology and working out what words mean. The dictionary and thesaurus online is a great way to understand the foundations of the word and look at options for words that mean the same thing but are more unique for your brand to use.

Find your One Word, then consider how that word becomes a simple way to explain the way you run your business, the way you present your brand, and what your brand stands for.

- Can you deliver on the One-Word brand promise in everything you do?
- Can you use that One Word to create a platform for your brand and business to revolve around?

"My brand One Word is: _____."

"Without knowledge action is useless and knowledge without action is futile."

~ Abu Bakr

Applying Your Brand True North

NOW YOU HAVE your compass to guide your brand and keep you on track:

- You know **WEST**: What is the problem you solve, for whom, and when it occurs, so you can identify exactly who is climbing your mountain.

- You know **EAST**: Your Expert-Ease, the unique way you approach what you do, your USP and how to explain your brand point of difference.

- You know **SOUTH**: Your value, the transformation you deliver, and the outcome people get from your brand.

- You know **NORTH**: The passion and purpose behind why you do what you do, the reason why your brand exists and the #1 thing your brand stands for.

It's time to use this brand direction to develop your marketing messages using the brand One Word to define how your brand makes people feel and clearly selecting images, colours, fonts, styles, and content that align with your brand core values.

Over the following chapters you will discover more about the science of neurobranding and how to apply it to your brand and your marketing. You will discover how to communicate Your Brand True North throughout all of your marketing, publicity, and promotional material.

This information is helpful if you want to:

- Start a new brand or rebranding,
- Create a personal brand to stand out as the expert,
- Align your personal brand with your business brand,
- Lead teams with confidence.

221

Some chapters will not be relevant to you, others will be incredibly useful. Feel free to read through and find what serves you best for your situation.

The Marketing Action Plan (MAP) will work for any of the above situations.

WHAT'S IN A NAME?

BROTHERS TOM AND JAMES are standing in the hot, cramped kitchen of the pizza parlour, and they are sweating. Tom has his hands on his hips, defiantly standing near the rear countertop, and James is leaning against the wall with his arms crossed. It's not just the heat of the pizza ovens that have them hot under the collar, it's the tension.

The owner of the pizza store and two others down the road, Dominick DeVarti, known as DomNick, is angrily gesticulating and expressing his rights. He is giving the brothers another history lesson and is flat refusing to agree to the deal. The whole business agreement hinges on the name.

James is ready to throw in the towel because he doesn't really want to give up his safe job at the post office anyway. *Just let him keep the business,* he thinks to himself, eyeing his brother Tom nervously and hoping to catch his attention so they can use this roadblock to back out of the deal.

Just then one of the pizza delivery boys slams open the back door and Jim jostles in with empty bags ready to fill the orders coming out of the oven. Jim realises he's stepped right into the middle of a row and as he sidesteps around the men heading to the collection area he hopes he hasn't been seen. He hears Dom shout in his thick Italian accent, "You can take my business but you can't take my name!"

Jim eavesdrops in on the heated discussion and continues to pack his bags. The stores are being sold! What will happen to his job? Will they stay pizza restaurants? Who will be the new boss? What is going on?

Eventually his bags are full and he knows he has to go back past the men to get to his delivery bike out the back door. As he rounds the countertop, Jim has an idea. He gathers his courage and pipes up, "Why not just call it Domino's Pizza?"

Fast forward to 1998 and Tom sells the business for $1 billion. In 2012 Domino's Pizza drops the word 'pizza' from the name, and now Domino's[xxviii] is one of the world's largest and most well-known pizza franchise brands. The three dots in the logo still signify the three original DomNick stores.

Today, everyone knows what Domino's sells and they all know the brand promise: Delivered on time or it's free.

Domino's is a word which never had anything to do with pizza. Many only knew of *dominoes*, the game to match the number of dots on little black blocks. When a delivery boy can come up with the solution for a brand name it should make you realise that creativity can come from anywhere.

When it comes to brand names and taglines, most professional services providers like to choose a name or a phrase that explains what they do, but it really isn't necessary or even a good idea to be so self-explanatory.

You might think it's important to have a brand name that describes your services, but you can choose a brand using that powerful science (neurobranding) that engages more emotionally with your prospect's brain.

You also do not need a tagline that explains what the business does. The purpose of a tagline is to connect with the prospect's brain and be memorable. A good tagline is clever, rhythmical, or has a double meaning and conveys a sense of the brand personality, value, and purpose.

When it comes to brand names and taglines, the best ones are short, catchy, and easy to adopt into everyday language.

Using neurobranding to create your brand name or tagline gives you a totally unique brand that actually means something without having to spell it out in black and white.

You might think a descriptive brand name is best because of your own innate desire to explain what you do. It's only human nature to want to be understood, and you probably want to stand out from the competition and may feel a descriptive brand name is the best way to do that. Yet the most iconic and easily recalled brand names do nothing to explain brand benefits and have massive recognition.

Leading technology companies seem to have gone fruity with Apple, Blackberry, and Orange for examples. These names have nothing to do with technology in the same way Twitter isn't just a noise birds make, and Uber isn't just a German word for 'over the top.'

It's also untrue that your brand name needs to be descriptive in order to be SEO-friendly. Originally, when the internet behaved like the Yellow Pages[66] and was more like a directory, having a URL that was searchable and easily findable was paramount. However, today all the web developers and SEO experts agree that search engine technology is far more advanced than just looking at the URL. SEO experts will tell you it is far more important to be consistent with quality keywords and focused quality within your content than having a brand name that includes a specific word.

Choosing a destination brand name may limit you to the location or region, unless your business is location-based, such as Boston Bakery or Plimmerton Plumber.

For professional services providers who struggle with brand names because they are selling the invisible instead of tangible

---

[66] The original source [in large books with lists of phone numbers] to find and connect with local plumbers, handymen, mechanics, attorneys, dentists, and more. —https://www.yellowpages.com/

products, it's so much more important to stand out because of your story rather than your location.

Some take the easy way out and name their business using their own name, but that's even riskier and not a clever way to create an asset or a meaningful brand. You might think using your own name to brand your business is a no-brainer, and although it appears to be a simple solution, in the long term using your own name makes it much more difficult to create a meaningful brand. What about Lorna Jane, Donald Trump, Pete Evans, or Coco Channel? I hear you say. Of course it has been done and there are well known name-based brands, but what may seem an easy way out at first, could create a rod for your own back.

The human brain 'sees' brands with emotion and attaches these to a memory in order to recognise and recall a brand when the need arises. When you use your name as your brand name any emotional connection is based on you rather than on a meaningful brand story. The fact is, if you use your name as your brand, that's it. End of story.

If your name is an aptronym[67], such as William Wordsworth who was a poet, Alexander G. Bell who invented the telephone, Mr. Crapper who invented the toilet, or like some of my friends who I am very envious of with their names such as Love, Brand, Power, and Perfect, you might be able to get away with it because the word means something more than just being a name.

When you use your name to brand your business there is little opportunity to create an emotional edge or give your target audience a reason to want to know more. When you use your own name for your brand name there is nothing more to say.

"Hi, I'm Joe Bloggs of Joe Bloggs and Associates." Nothing more to say and no questions are asked. There are however big

---

[67] aptronym: A name that fits a person's nature or occupation, like Jane House for a real estate agent

benefits and less risk if you avoid using your own name to brand your business.

The Biggest Risk of Using Your Name to Brand Your Business

You want your brand to become memorable for the right reasons. Benjamin Franklin once said, "It takes many good deeds to build a good reputation and just one bad one to lose it." When you brand with your name every public and private move affects your brand. By using your own name you could disenfranchise the very people you are trying to attract.

Donald Trump's brand once created an emotion of wealth and power, but as a political figure the Trump name has lost its shine. Lorna Jane created the emotion of vibrant fitness until the brand alienated women who aren't a particular shape and size. Celebrity chef Pete Evans healthy brand emotion now seems, quite frankly, a bit nuts. As for Coco Channel, the brand emotion is chic and classy but then, that wasn't actually her real name.

We are living in the age of authenticity where it's far too easy to find out what you are really all about and what you get up to.

When a company stuffs up, the PR team gets into action to manage the crisis. When the leader of a business stuffs up, suddenly it becomes personal. Now you have lost credibility and the shareholders are calling for your dismissal.

Personal brands that head up business brands like Richard Branson or who are responsible for the reputation of businesses which are not branded using their names, can focus on building the brand culture rather than on promoting their own name over that of their brand.

Janine Allis, founder of Boost Juice, once told me that personal branding was incredibly vital to her brand, so much so she avoids drinking alcohol in public because she can imagine the field day the press would have if she ever got caught drunk driving. "Juice Lady On The Juice," would be the headline in the papers and her worst nightmare.

Having your name out there as the go-to leader for what you do really well is great for referrals, but do you really want all that attention on your personal life?

There are of course examples of celebrities who have used their name to create a business, many of them TV stars. Ellen DeGeneres, Ed Sullivan, and Seinfeld, to name but a few.

The question to ask yourself is do you plan to spend many years and a great deal of money to build yourself into a celebrity brand, or would you rather spend your time making a great income helping people? From experience working with hundreds of professionals to develop a meaningful personal brand, it's going to take about three years for your brand to really get known. That's not a lot of time to get your own name to celebrity status where you have constant referrals, media interviews, and speaking requests from sources you didn't even know exist, just because they have heard of you.

Brand awareness takes time and you want to make sure you are investing in yours the right way, right from the start.

Even one of the most well-known personal brands who used her own name for her TV show, Oprah Winfrey, reversed her name to create a meaningful business brand and brand asset in HARPO.

The other risk of using your name for your brand is that you could end up losing your name or wishing you were no longer associated with the brand.

Brands named after people such as Hasbro, Disney, John West, and Kellogg's are now assets worth millions and live on longer than their namesakes. Most brand names are worth more than the actual company itself, and it is unlikely that a successful business will simply give you back your name, as Bobbi Brown discovered when she sold her makeup brand to Estée Lauder and was banned from using her own name[xxix].

The original founders of McDonald's[xxx] wished they hadn't sold their name to Ray Croc when he totally changed the culture and values of the brand, but it was too late and their name appears all over the world even though they disagreed with the business motives.

When Israel's health department ruled that Heinz tomato sauce could no longer be marketed as ketchup because it didn't have sufficient tomatoes in it[xxxi], Henry John Heinz would have turned in his grave. He purposefully put his sauces in glass bottles so consumers could see what was in them. He knew how to stand behind his brand values and offer transparency, but would probably be ashamed to have his name associated with the business today.

You never really know what the future will hold and where you or your business might end up. Tempting as it may be to brand with your own name when you provide a service (because you 'are' your business), it can minimise your brand growth and make you indispensable, and that's a problem if you want independence. Personal trainers, photographers, real estate agents, and business coaches who name their businesses after themselves have clients who expect them to show up at their door and no one else will fill their shoes. Like it or not, you generate a trust currency for your brand and when your company is named after you the only exchange clients want is engagement with you.

When your business is named after you, how do you add more team members or exit the business? If your brand is your name it's going to be difficult to cut yourself off from it when you need to. So go ahead and brand with your name but be prepared to front up. You are probably building your business to give you a lifestyle, so if you are considering branding with your name ask yourself what sort of life you want to have while you are building your brand.

You are welcome to brand your business with your name but be aware of the issues before you jump on the celebrity 'brand wagon.'

Creating a brand name might seem arduous but you can avoid the risks of using your own name and create definite benefits of having a meaningful brand name instead.

The Biggest Benefit of a Business Brand Name that isn't Your Own

A unique business brand name creates intrigue and tells a story that your ideal audience connects with.

It's stuffy in the brightly lit meeting room in spite of the blasting air conditioning as John lays his pen down on the notepad and rubs his forehead with his hand. *How much longer are these guys going to talk about nothing?* A business consultant, John has been called in to help this professional service provider who is at their wits' end. The cashflow has dried up, HR has a list of layoffs, the accountant is worried, and the boss's wife wants a divorce.

Among the arguments and discussions around the table which are going nowhere, John wonders *again* why they didn't call him in earlier. *Why did it take so long for them to ask for help?* It's almost too late now and it could have been different if they had gotten him in sooner.

John has struggled with this issue for a while. He always seems to be called in like an ambulance at the bottom of a cliff, with clients in such a bad way mentally that he has often suggested closing the business or even bankruptcy as a viable option, in order to save marriages and lives.

What can he do to be further up the food chain?

How can he position his brand as a means of positive help rather than a desperate rescue crew?

We discuss changing his business name from using his own name to a brand name, something he could play off to get in the door sooner, a brand that resonates with business owners and entrepreneurs who want to avoid hitting rock bottom, building a business rather than saving it.

John has just read a book about having a 'zero moment of truth' in life, a point where everything suddenly becomes real and you have your wakeup call, a point where you know you need to change something before it's too late.

BIZMOT, Business Zero Moment Of Truth is born.

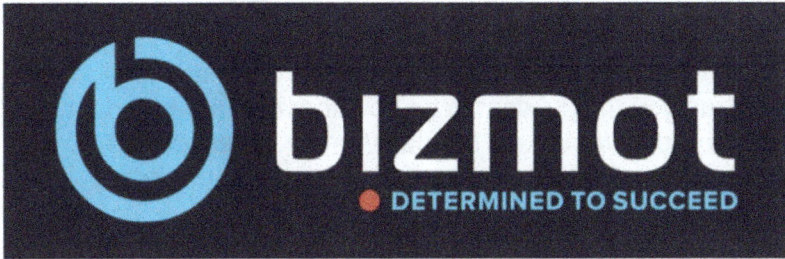

Now, instead of introducing himself as John Stringer Business Consultant, he finds himself explaining what BIZMOT stands for and how, having a zero moment of truth in business, is a good way to know you have to change things, before it's out of your control.

By having a brand name rather than using his own name he finds it much easier to share his brand story. People actually want to know what his brand name means, which is exactly what you want your brand to achieve—intrigue and interest, especially in a world where there is so much distraction and you have very little time to engage and connect with the right audience.

When you have a meaningful brand name that creates intrigue it opens the door to share so much more about who you are and your purpose and passion.

- What words mean something you want to be remembered for?

- Is there a word your brand could use to tell a story about your core passion?

- What words give the same impression you want your brand to communicate?

- How do you want to make people feel, and is there a word that has a double meaning that could do this for your business?

If you want to grow a successful business that can run without you, allowing you to focus 100 percent on the work you really love, without being the centre of attention, linking your growth, or appearing egotistical, you are best to choose a name that's not your own.

To really be successful you need your business to feed you, not to run you. If you want to be able to grow your brand and venture into new markets or add a variety of services, or franchise and duplicate yourself, a personally-branded business could hold you back and stifle your options.

Most importantly your brand is not actually that much about *you*. A brand comes from you but it is all about engaging and connecting with your ideal prospects and enabling them to know, like, and trust you from a simple interaction with your brand, without having to meet you.

Choosing a brand name is all about creating a brand that can 'speak' for you. A brand can do that if you are prepared to understand your target audience and build the subconscious triggers into your brand identity that instantly communicate with their brain, like Amazon, Nike, or FedEx.

If you still really want to use your own name in your branding, one option is to use it as an *endorsing brand*. ONE Active by Michelle Bridges is a clear example of brand extension which enabled a celebrity brand to branch out into the apparel market.

Or you can use your name to inspire the brand name. Adolf Dassler blended his name together to form Adidas[xxxii].

Brands help your brain make subconscious choices. An engaging brand name works hard to make it instantly easy for your ideal client to choose you. It might take a bit more effort, but you can create a meaningful brand name that enables you to have an emotional connection that sticks in your prospect's brain and has them asking more about your brand story.

So let's learn more about choosing a brand name and how you can have a brand that instantly tells a story.

CHOOSING A BRAND NAME

CHOOSING YOUR BRAND NAME is a challenge, and it does take focused effort to get it right, which is why branding agencies charge so much for this service. Before you decide you have found the right brand name, first check it is available with your country's company registration office. (In Australia this is ASIC and they have a quick brand name search available at https://businessname.com.au/.) You may also want to check the domain name (URL) is available, although having a .com is not as vital in the digital world today. A .net, .biz, .co, or even .me are all fine to use.

Having a name which is similar to your competitors' can make it harder to stand out, or you can ride on the coattail of an established brand by choosing something that sounds similar. An online brand we once launched was called Goodness & Gosh to compete alongside an established player in the same market, Villeroy & Boch.

One way to consider having a brand name that can be applied to multiple products or services, enabling growth and expansion, is to create an 'umbrella' brand. An example of this are car manufacturers, such as Toyota, Mazda, Ford. They are all umbrella brands for multiple sub-brands. The Ford Motor Company has Mustang, Falcon, Focus, Mondeo. All very different products with different audiences and budgets, but all falling under the same overarching brand name, Ford. With an umbrella brand you can create a brand name for an entire segment of the market.

Many brands you are familiar with come from the same company. Nestle and Unilever own hundreds of brands. Many of these brands compete against each other in the same market and have the same audience, such as coffee, chocolate, pet care, cosmetics, cereals, household goods. All different products but owned by the same company.

233

Have fun choosing a brand name. You can get really creative. The brand name doesn't need to describe the service or product nor does it need to be spelled correctly. For examples, Xero, Flickr, Froot Loops, Play-Doh, and Toys "R" Us are fine examples of brands that still make sense, even though they annoy the grammar police.

Branding is about engaging and connecting with your ideal prospects and enabling them to connect, resonate, and recall your brand from a simple interaction. Your brand name can do the engagement for you if you are prepared to understand your target audience and build the subconscious triggers into your brand identity which 'speak 'directly to their brain.

So let's make this easy. There are really only three formats for a successful brand name: descriptive, creative, or abstract.

Descriptive Brand Names

Brian Keen has been working with franchises for longer than he cares to remember, and knows all the success and failure stories. He has always approached life in a systematic way and loves processes but realises not many entrepreneurs are like him and that is what has led to so many problems in the past. He is sick of being contacted to help companies who have tried using the franchise model to grow their operations only to get into a huge mess. He really wants to be there right from the start, so the business can be organised with systems that enable duplication and sustainable growth.

He creates a 'business in a box' process that can be used to franchise almost any business model with a step-by-step program to ensure all the i's are dotted and the t's are crossed before things get out of hand. The Franchise Simply brand name says the right thing, but his logo doesn't truly paint the picture of how easy and ingenious his process is.

We work together to create a new identity that communicates not only how the brand delivers on its promise of simplicity, but also so people clearly understand how very easy it is to implement it once you have Brian's advice and process.

F & S of the brand name   Boxed system, simple to follow   Join the dots, uncomplicated duplication

Mel has a wellness clinic at her home and is providing an amazing service that delivers total transformation and changes lives. She has been working with the technology for a while now and is possibly the most experienced practitioner in the area by far, but her business is growing too slowly. She might be the expert, but no one knows it.

She feels something is missing from her branding. She likes the idea of helping people get their bodies back in alignment and into harmony, but that is hard to explain and it's not really igniting enough interest. As she takes a break between appointments and sips on her tea while rubbing the soft ears of her golden retriever that sits at her feet, she wonders, *What do my clients really want?*

We meet and go through the process of uncovering her brand story, identifying her ideal client, and how she wants the brand to make people feel. Love is one word she uses. She explains how they come to her downtrodden, tired and exhausted, and leave the clinic full of energy, bouncing out the door. "They feel great," she says to me. "I don't know how to explain it, but I give them energy."

I research the potential brand names and the brand Vivaciti is born. It is a word people know and understand, just spelt differently. It is what everyone wants and what everybody deserves.

Possibly the easiest way to create a brand name is to use words that describe what the product or service does. In fact many people say they prefer a brand that describes itself, but even though this is a viable brand name option, there is no actual evidence that a descriptive brand name increases recall.

Considering choosing a descriptive brand name derives from the fact that we often feel we need to explain things. The brain wants to identify the world around it and put things in boxes in order to feel safe. But consider some of the best-known brands. Few are descriptive.

Descriptive brands include the likes of:

- The Cheesecake Shop
- Carsales.com
- Baby Einstein
- Playmobil
- ColdPower
- Earth Choice
- Vaseline Intensive Care
- General Motors
- Kentucky Fried Chicken
- Toys "R" Us

Or the slightly more creative descriptive brand names that do tend to stand out a bit more:

- Kleenex
- Play-Doh
- Quick-Eze
- Ezi Office Supplies
- YoozUs

Of course, when it comes to explaining things to the brain, using words is not really necessary. Remember the bacon and eggs!

Brands like Vitafoam, BagCo, PlayStation are all okay brand names but they leave nothing to the imagination. By spelling it out you may have lost the opportunity to share your brand story, to connect and engage with ideal prospects.

There is also a problem if your business expands, the culture shifts, or you want to change direction. Can you continue to operate using a descriptive name if you no longer just do that?

Easy is not always best. Why not be more creative?

Created Brand Names

A created brand name can be totally unique and it can give you the ideal opportunity to share your brand story. Coca-Cola is possibly the most recognised product brand in the world and it's completely made up. John Pemberton originally made an alcoholic drink called French Wine Coca[xxxiii]. It was registered in 1885, but prohibition laws prevented him from selling it so he created a non-alcoholic version. When it came to naming, his partner and bookkeeper, Frank Robinson suggested the name Coca-Cola for the syrup formula: Coca from the coca leaves and Cola from kola nuts, changing the K to a C so it looked better.

Another example is Lego[xxxiv], one of the most famous product brands on the planet. Lego is derived from the Danish words 'leg godt,' meaning 'play well,' and it is easily recognised and recalled.

Isn't it interesting that with a created brand name you have a ready-made brand story. Something to create an interest and for people to learn about, understand, and share.

Evelyn gracefully floats into the room like a swan. Dressed impeccably, she glances around the room with a soft confidence and warmth that immediately puts people at ease. She feels, however, that she is much more like a swan than people actually know, calm and serene on top of the water and paddling like mad underneath the surface. Evelyn's personal brand is aligned with all things health and wellbeing. Having survived the trauma of having her husband go to jail for his financial misdeeds and losing everything before having to start again from nothing, she turned her life around and has created her own business, Aquarian Age Yoga.

The brand has served her well and helped her get on her feet again, but she has evolved since then and practices so much more than yoga now. She has many more services to offer and knows her brand is restricting her livelihood and holding her back.

We work together to find a brand identity that fits with her strategy and her personality. She sees so many stressed people trying so hard to chase fulfilment from the wrong sources. She worries that the world has too much stress, and feels that technology and many of the products we use are not helping us as much as we think they are. Her mission is to help people have a calmer life.

Qalma is created with the knowledge that it can be heard in different ways and mean different things. Karma, calmer, Qalma, it creates intrigue and meaning at the same time.

Green	calmness, growth, nature, nurture, health, natural, wealth
Purple	Healing, magic, service, luxury, wellness, mystery, holistic, encompassing

Yoga Pose

Water droplet
fresh, calm, restorative

Flame - life, energy, light

Tao symbol
The unclosed circle = life force

Having a meaningful name is more than having a descriptive name. It's about weaving intrigue, storytelling, and insight into the purpose behind the brand and into the name.

Created names can easily become eponyms, words that are used in everyday language like Frisbee and Hoover, very powerful brands that own an entire category and take on a powerful place in our vernacular and have become verbs. Hang on while I fill the Thermos! Created brands also tend to be short, sharp, and easy to recall, many with unusual spelling, such as OMO, XEROX, VISA, IKEA.

So, go ahead and have some fun. Think about how your business, service, or product was developed, what it means to you, what it's made of, what it does, how it works. Then create a brand name that you can tell a story about.

Abstract Brand Names

Despite the almost desperate determination to have a brand name that explains what your business does, or at least have a name that is created specifically for the brand, there are so many incredibly well-recognized and respected brands that have names with zero association to their product. In fact most of the best brand names are those you would never relate to the company at all:

- Dove: A bird or a range of cosmetics and body care products?
- Apple: A fruit or a phone, computer, or watch?
- Domino's: A game or a pizza?
- Puma: A ferocious beast or a sports shoe?

The coolest part about an abstract brand name is that people are almost compelled to want to know your brand story. An abstract name automatically creates intrigue. Nike is a great example of an abstract brand name that creates meaning, now that you know it's origin story. The brand has now taken on a life of its own and the brand identity can be communicated in one simple tick.

These incredibly well-known brands are easy to identify, even though their brand name is unrelated, because they are simple, short, catchy, and easy to pronounce so the brain loves them even though they are theoretically used out of context. Abstract names are ideal brand names if you want to weave a brand story (like Nike) into your marketing, website, collateral, and social media.

These incredibly well-known brands in this category, such as Virgin, are easy to identify because they have a double meaning. Richard Branson and his business partner Nik Powell decided to call the record store that they opened 'Virgin' because they were so new to business[xxxv]. The brand name now extends to all manner of services and products but the same culture remains where everything the brand does is unsullied by hidden agendas. The brand culture is that of 'look after the staff and they will look after the customers,' and there is something pure about that approach.

Play around with ancient languages or Greek mythology like Nike, the goddess of victory, and find a name that tells your brand story and creates emotion. Consider your origin story to see what feelings, emotions, or words stand out like a virgin.

Marguerita is excitedly catching up with people she hasn't seen in ages. Attending the networking event dressed in her usual attire of bright colours and high heels, the diminutive fireball conceals a secret talent not many know about. Yet.

As an opera singer she has honed her voice and practiced her breathing for years but she has recently discovered her singing skills have an even deeper purpose. Sound-healing. She has been learning everything she can about becoming a lightworker, using her voice to heal people, and the results so far from her work with clients in her online group have been incredible. She is so excited about how they are breaking through barriers and knocking down walls that have held them back for so long.

Her dream of changing the world and creating massive positive impact is coming true.

Trouble is her branding now doesn't match how she wants to make people feel. She launched the Conscious Wealth Institute some time ago in the hopes that she could begin a global movement while helping people rid themselves of self-worth issues. But so often though she finds those being attracted to her consultancy are not exactly ready for the power of her message. She is small but feisty, and her brand is all about calling people on the BS they have created for themselves and helping them muzzle their negative self-talk.

How can she communicate a stronger message that attracts the right people who are ready to not only listen but do something to change their lives?

We have a number of discussions and she discovers her new brand name which is the polar opposite of her current brand,

PitBull Mindset. We create a logo that is bright, colourful like her, and has the ferocity required to get her brand message across.

You can use words that have nothing to do with your industry or expert area but have a double meaning or tone that you know will work well to communicate how you want your brand to make people feel.

Be careful to have a brand name that is not too long, however. You will be tempted to shorten your brand name, to an acronym using initials, and that is not an ideal brand name for a number of reasons. The main reason is that initials do not tell a story and they can be confusing (Remember how Western Farmers Insurance looked like a WIFI provider?).

You may wonder why acronyms are not a good idea for a brand given IBM, ANZ, UPS, and a host of other brands that do exactly that, but remember what I said about the importance of generating an emotion with your brand? How can three letters of a brand name generate any sort of emotion?

Acronym brands take a long time to become established, to the point where you don't need to know what the initials stand for in order to understand what the brand stands for. Acronym brands actually don't want you to care what the initials stand for, they are happy for you to recall the short number of letters because they stand for much longer names.

Let's see if you can identify a few acronym brand names when they are spelt out:

- Minnesota Mining and Manufacturing Company (3M)
- Bavarian Motor Works (BMW)
- Dalsey, Hillblom, and Lynn (DHL)
- Entertainment and Sports Programming Network (ESPN)
- Mars & Murrie (M&Ms)
- Water Displacement 40th formula (WD40)
- Yet Another Hierarchical Officious Oracle (YAHOO)

Remember, the brain doesn't think in words, it thinks in pictures, and it's just too difficult to instantly convey a brand essence with an acronym, especially when you are starting out in business, so avoid using initials if you can.

The most important factor in choosing a brand name is to create meaning, for you, for your ideal client, and for their brain.

Above all, just remember that brands help your prospect's brain make subconscious choices. An engaging brand name and brand identity, using the right imagery and colours, can do a lot of the work for you, generating an emotional connection that makes it instantly easy for your ideal customers to choose you or your business.

Take the time to consider all three types of brand name and make a long list of options. Remember to stop and consider all of the created, abstract, and descriptive ideas.

Don't get too bogged down in the detail and make sure you are looking all around for the perfect opportunity to find your brand name.

It's a beautiful Sunday afternoon and the steep track into the gully is overgrown and muddy from last night's rain. We can hear the river below but are still descending down into the valley. The trees are providing a delightful respite from the hot midday sun and I'm looking forward to a soak in the pools at the bottom. Leaves cover the ground as we finally step down the rocky path to the riverbed. Up ahead we see the tiny metal swing bridge crossing the stream. It's here that we find we are not alone, many others have decided today is a good day for a bush walk too.

After a break at the river and a bite to eat we pull on our socks and tie up our shoes, looking skyward to the hilly path we now have to climb to get back up out of the gorge. As we cross back over the swing bridge and begin our climb, more people arrive at the swimming hole and cheerfully greet us as we pass them. "Keep an eye out for the koala," one man says to us.

Oh, how exciting, a koala in the wild! I wonder, *Where is it?*

Koalas are native to Australia and an iconic animal like the kangaroo that signifies the country, but they are becoming more and more endangered as developments take their native habitat. They are also motley in colour and camouflage well with the trees they live in. To see one in the wild is not something everyone can do. On our way back up the track we continuously scan the tree line, checking up every eucalyptus tree that looks even remotely like a good place for a koala to rest.

About 700 meters from the start of the track, I suddenly look up directly above the path and there it is on a branch, only a few meters above our heads, a koala, sleeping in the crook of the tree! *How on earth had we missed seeing it on our way down?*

It's very much like that as a business leader or entrepreneur. We are heading down watching what's going on, and are too busy focusing on the vital to-do's on our list to notice the world around us. We spend so much time and effort concentrating on what we have to do, chasing those bright, shiny objects, like seeking the rewards of the refreshing swim after the long trek, that we often miss seeing perfect opportunities right in front of us.

That's why, now that you have Your Brand True North compass that keeps you on track, you can be more creative, clever, and exploratory. You can have some fun being adventurous in delivering your brand, choosing a name, or creating marketing that has real direction and brings your ideal clients back to your brand. Now you have everything you need to create a stand-out brand with meaning and purpose.

- You have direction for your brand strategy and a clear focus on what makes your brand unique.

- You know how your personal brand aligns with the business brand.
- You know where you are positioned with a band compass firmly pointing towards your True North.

It's time to create a Marketing Action Plan (MAP) to follow.

MARKETING
ACTION
PLAN

MARKETING ACTION PLAN

BUILDING A STRONG brand is like building a strong body. Just like paying an expensive gym membership and then never going, you can spend plenty on a brand identity, a website, or collateral, but if you don't leverage it you simply won't get seen and noticed. You have to put in the reps. You have to be consistent in order to see the results. Imagine a brand is like a gym and marketing is like regularly showing up. The more you go and the more effort you put in, the better you look and the stronger your brand grows.

Leveraging a brand with consistent marketing includes:

- Consistently sharing your message,
- Writing blogs,
- Keeping your website up-to-date,
- Being regular on social media with relevant content,
- Guest speaking or being interviewed on podcasts,
- Going after new business,
- Following up using the collateral you invested in,
- Making your mark with targeted media,
- Advertising,
- Publicity,
- Attending networking activities,
- Belonging to memberships, groups, and associations.

Yes these are all things you might find daunting and difficult, but they all help your brand get seen and noticed, gaining credibility, and the more you do them the more memorable your brand becomes.

Just like starting a new gym, tentatively poking your head around the corner, quietly stepping in the door and timidly watching all the fit people sweating it out, lifting weights or doing exercises you think are impossible, putting yourself out there is initially challenging. But after you take the first few steps and the more you are prepared to learn and keep doing the hard stuff, it does become easier. You will eventually get the results you really want. A stand-out brand and a business that gets amazing reviews and recommendations is just like having a fit and healthy body people compliment you for. The effort is definitely worth it.

One way to make it easier when you join a gym is to have a goal and to know what you want to get out of your membership. That way the coaches and trainers can help you achieve this by setting you programs and plans to suit you.

It's the same when it comes to leveraging your brand message to deliver your marketing. Now that you have a brand promise you developed with your compass, it is time to deliver on those promises with everything you and your business do.

Your Brand Promise

MAKING SURE YOU deliver on your brand promise keeps your marketing on track and gives everyone in the business a guide to keep them on True North.

In her little green shop in Brighton, Anita is busy stocking the shelves and refilling customers' containers. She is exhausted but happy that more people seem to be finding their way to her door.

It has been so much hard work to get the store open. Sourcing the products she knows are not tested on animals was hard enough, and she can't count how many hours were dedicated to researching, calling suppliers, and trying to source enough bottles. She smiles to herself and shakes her head, knowing she never did manage to get enough recyclable bottles but thanks to her brainwave in the middle of the night, the 'refill your own container' idea certainly seems to be working.

Anita sighs as another customer enters the store. She sees their eyes light up as they breathe in the cacophony of aromas from the soaps, and enjoys every moment of their animated facial expressions while they read the stories behind each bar.

At least I know this is a good product, she thinks to herself. No matter how much of a success the shop is, Anita can sleep soundly at night knowing she is doing something, no matter how small, to change the world.

The Body Shop[xxxvi] eventually sells to L'Oréal for $820 million.

Anita's brand promise was sustainability, harmony, and principal over profit. Anita always had a personal passion for the planet and was constantly campaigning for causes so even when her business grew to almost 2,000 stores worldwide, the brand stayed true to the Brand True North. The brand core value of being a force for good was embedded in the brand promise and everything they did delivered on that, from the way they sourced, manufactured, and packaged their products to the sponsorships and charities they supported. They even developed a doll that

249

was a more usual looking shape and size to help redefine how girls saw beauty. Ruby was one of their most successful marketing campaigns.

Anita even once said, "We knew about storytelling then, so all the products had stories. We recycled everything, not because we were environmentally friendly, but because we didn't have enough bottles. It was a good idea. What was unique about it, with no intent at all, no marketing nous[68], was that it translated across cultures, across geographical barriers, and social structures. It wasn't a sophisticated plan, it just happened like that."

If you have your brand well and truly pointing True North, your marketing messages and even the way you deliver on your promises will come naturally.

Express service provider DHL sponsors surf lifesaving[xxxvii] which delivers on the brand promise of being speedy. Red Bull[xxxviii] continued from the very early days of appearing at Muay Thai venues to sponsoring extreme sports arenas and athletes around the world, which reinforces their high-octane energy brand promise. Domino's Pizza deliver on their guarantee, 'On time or it's free.'

Be careful to choose a brand promise you can deliver on. A good brand promise has three vital elements:

- **Deliverable**: You can actually deliver on the promise, it's not just something that sounds good but has no way of ever being accomplished.

- **Measurable**: You can check it is working with reviews, ratings, or results. You can measure if it has value or is building brand awareness or increasing profits.

---

[68] nous, (Greek: "mind" or "intellect") in philosophy, the faculty of intellectual apprehension and of intuitive thought. —https://www.britannica.com/topic/nous

YOUR BRAND TRUE NORTH

- **Meaningful**: It fits with the brand core values and has a purpose. Not just something that sounds good, it can be a mantra used within your entire business.

Yvon is cold. He's been rock climbing all day with his friends and it was great while the sun was out, but now it's getting dark and the air temperature has dropped so fast he is shivering. They told him it was colder in Scotland than he was used to in the U.S.A., but he didn't really think it would get this cold. He checks his wallet to see how much money he has made from selling the environmentally friendly climbing gear he makes, and decides he might have enough to go into town to get something warmer to wear.

In a shop in the village he finds something called a rugby jersey and deciding the fabric looks tough enough to handle the conditions, he buys one with the last of his funds. The next day it's still cold, so he climbs wearing the jersey and notices how the broad collar of the shirt stops the climbing slings from cutting into his neck. He has an idea.

Yvon starts buying and selling jerseys, sourcing them from New Zealand and Argentina, but they sell out so fast he is always trying to get more. He starts selling other equipment, clothing, and tents, and eventually decides he needs his own brand. He also wants to fulfil his passion for causing no unnecessary harm and building on the entire reason he started making those climbing spikes right back when he first found out about rugby shirts.

Patagonia[xxxix] is now one of the world's leading environmentally-friendly clothing brands and is a business dedicated to finding a solution for the ongoing environmental crisis.

Now that you know how to really leverage a brand, you are ready to create a MAP (Marketing Action Plan) to stay consistent and surround all of those prospects who are climbing your mountain. Now that you have a brand compass and you know the position of your brand and what you want to be known for, it's time to have a MAP so you can avoid knee-jerk reaction style marketing.

DEVELOP YOUR MAP

A MAP gives you a strategy to follow and helps you be sustainable with your marketing activity. Your ideal prospect is currently lost in the woods with so many marketing messages bombarding their brain, while they try to find a way up the mountain of their pain to get to a solution. If you can surround them with a consistent message and be present when they most need you, your brand will be the one they choose ahead of the competition.

You know that recognisable brands who have great reputations and are respected as leaders have more market share. There is a reason for that—*recall*. Great brands know that if they imbed the brand into the mind of a potential client this will help with brand recollection when it comes time to buy. Just consider the last time you really wanted a particular make and model of vehicle. Once you had decided you wanted the latest BMW (or whatever), did you suddenly notice more of them around you? Did you see the dealerships on the corner or the billboards or adverts?

The likes of Facebook and Instagram have ways of stalking you and we all believe Google and Siri are listening, but in reality your brain is also working hard to make marketing messages more relevant to you. It's called *reticular activation*[69]. Those 5,000 branded messages a day can't all possibly be absorbed, and your brain has been very busy filtering out all the stuff you don't need to know or notice. Once you decide you want something your brain automatically removes the filter and starts to bring that

---

[69] The Reticular Activating System (RAS) is a bundle of nerves at our brainstem that filters out unnecessary information so the important stuff gets through. The RAS is the reason you learn a new word and then start hearing it everywhere. It's why you can tune out a crowd full of talking people, yet immediately snap to attention when someone says your name or something that at least sounds like it. —https://medium.com/desk-of-van-schneider/if-you-want-it-you-might-get-it-the-reticular-activating-system-explained-761b6ac14e53

thing to your attention. It is the same with brand recognition and recall.

Those dealerships and adverts for BMWs were always there, your brain just filtered them out. The minute you became interested in them, your brain pointed out where you could solve your pain or problem or manifest your desire.

Of course it is going to take concerted time and effort to surround your audience and be chosen as the leading brand. As a busy business owner it is impossible to maintain this unless you have a system that enables you to implement your brand strategy. And you need an easy way to create the right sort of content that gets noticed by the right prospects, like putting up a signpost that has exactly the right message in the right place to lead them your way.

Here are some tips to help you create your Marketing Action Plan.

Set a BHAG—a Big Hairy Audacious Goal

Knowing what you really want your brand to be known for means you can set goals for the year and break them down into monthly, weekly, and even daily action steps:

- How many clients do you want to have, spending how much, buying what?
- Which podcasts or stages are going to get you in front of the right audience?
- Which media would you like to be featured in that will boost your brand awareness?
- Who are the influencers you want to get your brand in front of and where are they hanging out?

Just like starting out at the gym, if you just want to lose 10 kg or compete in bodybuilding, those are two very different goals and require different action steps.

Either way, set goals that scare you a bit and seem a bit out of reach right now. This will help you keep focused and motivated and will enable you to achieve small goals that will make you want to reach the bigger goals ahead.

Personalise the Plan

Your MAP is not a to-do list that just joins all the other scraps of paper or notes in your diary. Just like trying to lift too much weight and injuring yourself at the gym, if you don't make your marketing manageable you will give up. Avoid overwhelming yourself by creating an action plan for your marketing activity each week.

Fill the weekly plan with set tasks that will build your brand profile. In the same way a personal trainer would create a personalised plan for your fitness, start to write out the activities to do and when they will occur, scheduling them into your week so they become part of your routine.

Choose the Right Activity

Just like losing those winter kilos or creating a summer body, business is seasonal. You can 'high-jack' current topics to create relevant and newsworthy content so your audience will get more engagement and you will get better results:

- When do you have a summer sale?
- When do you start promoting Christmas gifting?
- When should you launch a back-to-school promotion, or end-of-fiscal-year (EOFY) special?

Planning ahead and creating opportunities to get seen and noticed means you are surrounding your ideal audience at a time when they most need and want your services or products. Retailers know how to do this well. Just look in the shops to see when they start promoting Mother's Day. I guarantee it's at least a month before the date. We all see hot cross buns in the shops just after Christmas and Easter Eggs appearing in February, even though Easter isn't until March/April. They never leave it to last minute, they extend the promotion period to make the most of it.

You can also leverage vital dates such as your business anniversary or a seasonal promotion specific to your industry. Fishing and camping stores have duck or bear shooting season sales. Pubs leverage St. Patrick's Day to serve up Guinness and paint the town green.

You can also leverage historical events, anniversaries of interest, and celebrity birthdays that mean something to your business.

We are looking at celebrity birthdays to find marketing ideas for a BBQ brand and are checking through the birthdays of celebrities this month to see what we can find. We do a Google search on the celebrities' names and the word barbecue to see what comes up. Elon Musk[70]'s birthday is on the 28th June. What on Earth can he have to do with BBQs? Turns out people are using his famous flamethrowers[xl] to cook meat and we have a story to tell on social media that we know will be captivating, interesting, and click-worthy.

Your brand can create a following by simply being relevant. Do your research, find content that creates intrigue and links back to your brand message, share some insight, and then link your post back to an article on your website.

Show Up

Allocate at least one hour a week to work on your business marketing. One hour minimum. In one hour you could write a blog for your website and email the link to your customers. You could write an article and send it to an industry publication or find a

---

[70] Elon Reeve Musk FRS born June 28, 1971) is a business magnate and investor. He is the founder, CEO, and Chief Engineer at SpaceX; angel investor, CEO, and Product Architect of Tesla, Inc.; founder of The Boring Company; and co-founder of Neuralink and OpenAI. —https://en.wikipedia.org/wiki/Elon_Musk

podcast to feature it on, or post a podcast interview link on LinkedIn.

Too much too soon? Not sure you have it in you to be that creative? How about writing a social media post about just one of the initiatives your brand is taking, how you overcame a challenge, won an award, or hired a new team member? Share how you launched a new service or product or simply share a recent case study, review, or testimonial you received. There is nothing better than a bit of third-party credibility to help your brand stand out.

Or how about telling your own origin story? Just like the before and after weight loss journeys we see at the gym, imagine the engagement if you could share a story of when you started your business, or what you were doing to build your brand a year or so ago, and what you are doing now.

Be Accountable

Find a business buddy, like a gym buddy, and catch up each week on the phone by email or have a coffee and share what you have achieved. Then set goals for the next week.

Having someone to train in the gym with is the best way to stay motivated and positive. That way you won't both quit on the same day. There will be times you want to let fear stop you and your business buddy will help you overcome your concerns because you just want each other to succeed. With a business buddy you can share the load and work together. Interview each other to share a relevant topic and submit it as an article to a magazine, broadcast it as a podcast, or go on and do a live Zoom or Facebook video together.

The most important thing to remember is that maps and compasses are old technology. They have been used for many centuries and they are old school. There is a reason why this book is not called *Finding Your Brand GPS*.

No matter what new technology, social media, or latest craze like TikTok, Periscope, or Clubhouse, human beings are driven by the same needs and wants. Our brains operate the same way they did when we were cavemen and women. We are emotional beings and we buy on instinct.

The brand creates the feelings, the marketing delivers the message. The channel you use to reach your potential clients and customers is just that. A channel. One of many. Like a road leading to a village or a pathway to a town, social media, traditional media, direct marketing, advertising are all ways to get your message out there. You don't have to be on all of them.

If you are accountable to your brand promise and your marketing message is aligned with Your Brand True North, it is easy to choose the right direction.

Misguided By Media

WE ARE OCEAN RACING from the Gold Coast[71] to Julian Rocks[72] on a 50-foot carbon-fibre racing yacht called Cyclone. The 15 amateur crew are all set for a very long 85 nautical mile race that started at 11 a.m. and won't finish until the wee small hours of the next day. An 'overnighter 'with gear, food, supplies, safety equipment, and everyone working in shifts. It is sunny but the forecast doesn't look that flash. There's a prediction of a large storm in the afternoon and as the day progresses things don't bode well.

The trip south has been uneventful and everyone is in a positive mood. We are making quite good headway hitting 10 knots at times and rotating the helm. After many hours the jagged spikes of Julian Rocks eventually appear on the horizon but as we near them the sky gets dark and the wind begins to drop.

It is the calm before the storm.

We settle in and the decision is made to have an early dinner of pre-prepared risotto and rolls while we wait for the wind to come back. We are becalmed, replete, and looking at our turning point of the small rocky formation just off the coast in Byron Bay, which is only a hundred metres or so ahead of us, but we are going nowhere fast and an ugly black sky is growing increasingly large in front of us.

---

[71] The Gold Coast is a coastal city in the state of Queensland, Australia, approximately 66 kilometres (41 mi) south-southeast of the centre of the state capital Brisbane and immediately north of the border with New South Wales. — https://en.wikipedia.org/wiki/Gold_Coast,_Queensland

[72] The Julian Rocks Nguthungulli Nature Reserve is a protected nature reserve that is located on the Julian Rocks in the Northern Rivers region of New South Wales, in Australia. The 4,047-hectare (10,000-acre) reserve comprise two small islands, situated approximately 2.5 kilometres off the coast of Byron Bay. —https://byronbay.com/julian-rocks/

We sit there for almost 45 minutes before a huddle forms between the skipper, the helm, and the most experienced of the crew, who toss about options as to what we should do.

The decision is made: safety first, and the 'iron spinnaker' (or engine for the landlubbers[73]) is turned on. We tack about and head home, pulling out of the sailing race without rounding the rocks. We keep a wary eye on the fast-approaching storm hoping we can outrun it.

We don't.

The storm hits with such ferocity that most of the crew head below and only the experienced sailors take turns to helm and keeping watch. The last of the sunlight disappears and the rain begins to pelt down on us like a never-ending waterfall. Visibility is abysmal and unbeknown to us, the rain is hitting with such force that the drops landing on the navigation screen change our position.

I am helming through the deluge as the darkness closes in on us. Staring into the blackness I check my instruments and maintain the heading I have been given. Or at least I think I am. I start to hear something on the port side of the boat. It sounds like waves, *but how can it be? We are out at sea.* I shake off the noise I think I hear and go back to trying to stay on course, peering into the darkness, watching the screen, and keeping us headed south.

There it was again. . . What was that noise?

I rip off the hood of my waterproof jacket, caring less about the rain in my face and more about that sound. *It is waves! And they are crashing just off the port side of the boat!"*

A shout comes from below where a crew member has fired up the extra iPad in the dry environment of the cabin, "Get off the beach!"

---

[73] landlubber: noun, an unseasoned sailor or someone unfamiliar with the sea. —https://www.dictionary.com/browse/landlubber

"Going about!" I quickly call. I turn 90 degrees to starboard and we start heading out to sea again. The beach the waves are breaking on is Kingscliffe[74] and we had been within only a few hundred metres of it. The fact that we were so close to danger even though I had technology right in front of me that said otherwise scares the crap out of me.

From then on in we use the old fashioned compass which, encased in its plastic dome, is impervious to the rain smashing down on us.

As it turns out this is one of the worst storms in 100 years with some of the highest rainfalls that had ever been recorded in such a short timeframe.

After a very long, wet, dark journey we arrive safely back at the marina, all of us ready for warm showers and bed, but I am also more knowledgeable and wise for the experience.

The lesson is that we can rely on technology too much.

There are so many apps, channels, platforms, and online tools that make it easy to create our own marketing and promotional content, but if we don't know where we are going and what the end goal is, technology can make it even more overwhelming and confusing. Your marketing message can get lost in the wrong channel or it can lose its impact entirely if you let the platform direct the brand strategy.

For business, getting lost in the technology can get downright dangerous.

Before computers, the creatives at the advertising agencies I worked with first drew ideas before discarding those that didn't fit the brief. They kept going until they knew they had the best options that worked the best to get the result the client wanted.

---

[74] Kingscliff is a coastal town just south of Tweed Heads in the Northern Rivers region of New South Wales, Australia, and is a beach community offering a variety of holiday accommodations. — https://en.wikipedia.org/wiki/Kingscliff,_New_South_Wales

Only then would production begin and the ideas be made to look good. After that they were presented to the client for approval.

Even then the decisions were made based on, 'Does this answer the brief?. The ideas would be chosen based on how it was most 'on-brand' and taking the brand in the right direction. Much like our yachting adventure where we were off course and going in the wrong direction because we let technology lead the way, you can get side-tracked into creating all sorts of directionless activity instead of following the plan.

I see so many in business spend thousands on WOFTAM with endless photoshoots, shooting videos, creating content, designing memes and collateral, recording podcasts, or writing blogs that all have different themes, styles, and mixed messages. They get caught up in what the technology is capable of doing. It is exciting, fast and accessible, but has no strategy or consistency.

Your brand compass guides your marketing message and the technology enables you to broadcast it. When you have a brand strategy and direction to go, you can create a MAP to follow that includes the channels to use to reach your audience.

If you choose to ignore the brand promise and get caught up in the trends or technology it's easy to get overwhelmed. When a brand is at the mercy of the environment and relies too much on the tech, your marketing message can easily go in a wrong direction.

The first step for your Marketing Action Plan is to get clear on the brand message, then schedule your activity, and after that you can use all sorts of tools available to help you get the message out there. Remember, just because you can, doesn't mean you should.

When you are implementing your MAP check that it is a message that fits with your brand strategy and promise.

- Will it resonate?
- Is it the right place to share this message?

- Is it the right activity and channel to get the message to the right person at the right time?

Make sure when you create the content in your MAP that you are setting your direction and following the brand strategy. Don't get distracted by the bright-shiny-objectitis of the next cool channel, app, or program that comes your way.

If you set the intention of Your Brand True North with everything you do, it is easy to follow the Marketing Action Plan and you'll get your message where you want it to go.

Now that you have Your Brand True North and you know who you are targeting and what will engage and motivate them to know, like, and trust your brand and business, you can use your brand One Word to start creating your Marketing Action Plan.

With a brand strategy on True North and a MAP to follow, your content and marketing messages will naturally attract the right clients, investors, supporters, and even the right staff for your team.

As long as it matters to them.

LAUREN CLEMETT

MARKETING THAT MATTERS

INSIDE THE TUNNEL the noise of the crowd in the stadium is deafening. It's been months of planning and effort to get to this day and as brand manager for AXA, I get to lead the New Zealand Rugby Sevens team out onto the pitch for the opening of the tournament. I'm making sure my team of AXA staff members, resplendent in their bright blue AXA t-shirts, all have the correct country sign and are waiting in front of each team playing in the two-day tournament.

The Sevens have been a phenomenally popular event in New Zealand for a few years, with tickets selling out in hours and hundreds of people travelling from all over the country to attend. It's not so much about the rugby as it is about the party. Everyone is in dress-ups of some sort, many in costumes or role playing anything from the tan-coloured CHiPs[75] to the black robes of nuns and even a few Borats[76].

On the first night of the event it's a packed house, having filled quickly as the day progressed and people made their way to the stadium after work. The lights drop, music begins to rumble from the speakers in the roof of the circular arena, spotlights flood the green grass in front of us, and we are instructed to begin walking out.

As my crew lead the teams out to the middle of the rugby field they are smiling from ear to ear. I hope they enjoy every moment

---

[75] CHiPs is an American crime drama television series created by Rick Rosner, that originally aired on NBC from September 15, 1977, to May 1, 1983. It follows the lives of two motorcycle officers of the California Highway Patrol (CHP). — https://en.wikipedia.org/wiki/CHiPs

[76] Borat! Cultural Learnings of America for Make Benefit Glorious Nation of Kazakhstan (Kazakh / Russian: Борат) (also stylized as BORДT, or simply Borat) is a 2006 mockumentary black comedy film directed by Larry Charles and starring Sacha Baron Cohen. —https://en.wikipedia.org/wiki/Borat

of this because they have all worked so hard to leverage the sponsorship and get everything ready for this day.

The AXA brand is everywhere and there is good reason for that. My direction has been to increase brand awareness by at least 10 percent and I want the TV cameras to broadcast as much of that distinctive logo as possible.

The New Zealand team is last to enter the stadium as they are the hosts for this round of the year-long competition that travels around the world. I adjust my hat to make sure the AXA logo is front and centre, knowing the NZ TV cameras will be focused on capturing the home team as they enter at the opening ceremony.

Suddenly it's NZ's turn to exit and I am jostled to the front, grabbing the pole of the sign I will hold, and I look ahead to check on my team. But as I walk out into the open mouth of the tunnel and the team name is announced, the crowd goes absolutely nuts and my brain stops.

The hairs on the back of my neck stand up and any thought of managing my team is gone as I realise all eyes are on me leading the team out. The lights are blinding and the music blares as I try to remember to breathe.

There is a rush of adrenalin coursing through me and my palms sweat, making it difficult to hold up the sign above my head. I catch myself in awe of the moment and come to my senses. I take a gasp of air into my lungs that clears my head and put one foot in front of the other. As I lead the New Zealand team out I am watching where I am going and making sure I stand up straight and perform the task at hand.

So often as leaders we can get caught up in the running of the business or the daily tasks, we fail to revel in the moments where our leadership rewards us. When we lead we often put others first and it's only in exceptional moments that we realise how lucky we are to be doing what we love. However, when everything is in alignment the price of leadership pays off because that's when we really shine. This is why it is so vital you know why you are a leader, that you know your purpose, and where you want to position yourself. When your own personal brand aligns with the business brand, you will know you are in the right place.

Before we create a MAP so you can get out there with your brand message, promoting what you and your business does and what makes you the leader in your industry, first we need to make sure you are 100 percent clear on the meaning behind your marketing and how it can be connected to your brand promise as well as your personal brand values.

Remember your brand One Word?

• This is your brand strategy.

• It gives your message consistency and communicates Your Brand True North.

That's why it is so important to choose your One Word well.

Everything your Brand True North stands for, everything that comes from your brand One Word, needs to be instilled into your marketing message.

When your brand message has meaning it makes it easy for your promotion, advertising, or marketing to remain 'on-brand.'

When your personal brand aligns with the business brand, regardless of if you are the business owner or not, you have shared values that give you and your marketing message meaning and purpose. Because of this alignment you naturally care that the brand makes good on all of the promises it makes in the marketing messages. Your personal brand integrity supports the business brand honesty and vice-versa.

• If someone questions the business brand, they are questioning the business leadership.

• If the behaviour of the business leader contradicts the brand values, everyone notices the incongruence.

• If the marketing message undermines the brand promise, the marketplace questions the leaders capability.

We have all seen enough marketing mistakes to know that the first thing most people say is, "Who approved that?" You know your own personal brand reputation is on the line with every marketing campaign or promotion, so it's vital you care about how the brand message is marketed, and you have to cut through the noise of an overcrowded world to make it into the grey matter of your ideal prospect's brain.

Your marketing needs to matter, and you need to care that it does. Because if you don't mind, it doesn't *matter*!

You will save a lot of time and effort by considering if your marketing is aligned with the brand and if it provides substance to support and deliver on the brand promise for your audience *before* you create your message.

Here is a guide to help you ensure your content creation and marketing message matches Your Brand True North, and to make sure it matters to your customers. A Marketing Message That MATTERS™ stands for:

- **M**eaningful: Not just 'Buy my stuff,' your message has a purpose. We all know what it's like to be sold to or to be sucked in by clickbait headlines that let you down and waste your time. Don't be flippant or sneaky. Be engaging, fun, and relevant. Consider if it is meaningful to your ideal client. Would they find it helpful? Would it deliver something meaningful to them? Does the marketing deliver on the brand promise?

- **A**ctivates: Your message should elicit some sort of action or answer a need or question. It could help increase awareness, drive sales, entice a following, or invite engagement, educate, build trust, introduce a new service or product. When you create your marketing you need to know what you want your audience to do as a result of it.

- **T**rending: The media call this *newsjacking*, sharing or posting something that relates to a recent news story or topic that people are already talking about. If you set up Google alerts about your industry you can get automated emails sent to you so you can share relevant articles, opinions, or your viewpoints on topics. This way your marketing creates the perception that your brand is up with the play and that you are a market leader.

- **T**ruthful: Brands that deliver on their promises tell honest stories, not just fluff or 'polishing a turd' by glossing over what's really going on. We are living in the age of authenticity and people want to know who is behind the business. People buy from people, so share your challenges as the leader as well as the business success. Give people an insight into your beliefs, values, passions, and real feelings. If you make mistakes be honest. Yes, you are a leader but let them know you are human, too.

- **E**motive: People buy with emotion and justify with fact. The brain really loves a good story, so don't just highlight the benefits or features of your products or services, engage with emotion. Share case studies, testimonials, jokes, tales, and lessons you and the team have learnt. Use creative language and expressions, colourful or rhyming phrases, and phrases or particular smells and sounds that will lodge in the hearts and minds of your ideal clients and make your marketing memorable.

- **R**esonate: Your marketing message should meet your audience where they are, connecting with the brain and the heart of your ideal prospect. Consider the pain they are in and why they need your services or products before trying to sell to them. Put yourself in their shoes and use language, words, and images that will help them see themselves in your marketing messages.

- **S**ensible: Sure, have fun, be irreverent, or even controversial. As long as the marketing message aligns with the brand personality, values, and beliefs it will make sense to your raving fans and loyal clients. Use relevant dates in your promotional calendar and have promotions that are timely and valuable. Consider what times of the year your brand is most needed—school holidays, winter, ready for Christmas. Pick the right time to share a Marketing Message That MATTERS™.

Now let's create a MAP for you to follow.
You can download a Marketing Action Planner here:

www.yourbrandtruenorth.com/MAP

USING YOUR MAP

Marketing Action Plan

JUST LIKE A MAP which shows the contours of the land and where the roads and places of interest are, a Marketing Action Plan gives you a system to follow. It helps you plan ahead, knowing what to do and where to put the signposts that promote your brand to make sure you are surrounding your ideal client.

Remember *reticular activation* and how your brain brings things of interest to your attention? Having a MAP helps give your brand the visibility to make sure it is the one people choose when they most need or want your product, service, or leadership.

Let's take it one step at a time.

Step 1: Set Your Brand Strategy

Your One Word.

Yes, I know I am harping on about how vital it is but if you haven't got it yet now is the time to choose one. Once you have your brand One Word, everything you do on your MAP will flow from that.

- Write your One Word at the top of your MAP.
- Use the thesaurus to collect as many words that mean the same as your One Word.
- Find quotes and phrases that communicate the feeling of your One Word.
- Create a list of descriptive terms you can use in your marketing that amplify your brand. Consider idioms and repeatable phrases, commonly used sayings and quotes that will get recalled, remembered, and retold.

I have a list of around 100 phrases to do with *direction* (my One Word), everything from making marketing a walk in the park to staying on track.

What are some sayings you can use that have something to do you with your brand strategy?

This treasure trove of content-generating ideas can be used to reinforce your brand message without using the same words over and over again. It keeps your marketing message fresh but still on track with your brand strategy.

Step 2: Choose Themes

Find the themes for each month. Consider activities or events that are already taking place. What are the seasons, holidays, celebrations, or festivities your audience is aware of and participates in?

- Winter warmers?
- Mother's Day?
- Spring break?
- Christmas?
- Valentine's Day?

You already know what topic most people are going to be interested in during the year, so go with the flow and news-jack them by basing your marketing message each month on a relevant theme. If you have months where there are no obvious themes you can create themes based on your brand message you know your audience will be interested in.

For example:

- End of financial year for accounting,
- School term starting for stationery providers,
- Summer holidays for travel agents,
- Spring for pool cleaning companies.

At all times consider what your ideal client is going through that your brand helps them with the most. There are plenty of examples of brands who have 'news-jacked[77]' themes as thinly disguised bait to win followers or make sales (such as homeware brands newsjacking hurricane season). Their cleverness was inconsistent or insensitive and they got caught out and complained about, and it can happen to you.

Remember, your marketing needs to *matter*.

- What does someone need for their home in winter that doesn't happen in summer and vice-versa?

- When looking for a consultant do they need advice and help to start something, manage and grow it, or exit the situation?

- Are they buying a second hand car for themselves? A new car? Or a car for their daughter?

- Looking for gifts for others or buying for themselves?

Before you newsjack anything, consider what is going on in and around your prospect's life at different times during the year and when it might be best to help them with a certain topic. Plot the themes out for all months.

For example, a Marketing Action Plan for a dog grooming business might have a blog about winter coats and that 'wet dog smell' in July for the southern hemisphere, and in February for the Northern hemisphere. During that month you may discover that it's a celebrity's dog's birthday, or the anniversary of the release of a dog film like *Lassie*.

Here is an example of the themes of a MAP for a success coaching business for women, based in Australia (when summer is December-February and Winter is June-July):

- **January:** New Year new you, goal setting

- **February:** Valentine's Day, the month of love or luck, St. Patrick's Day

---

[77] Newsjacking is the practice of aligning a brand with a current event in an attempt to generate media attention and boost the brand's exposure. — https://www.techtarget.com/searchcontentmanagement/definition/newsjacking

- **March:** Easter, new beginnings, creating something new
- **April:** April Fool's Day, don't get misled
- **May:** Mother's Day, looking after yourself
- **June:** Imposter syndrome, how to back yourself
- **July:** Mid-winter blues, EOFY, financial goals for the year
- **August:** Women's equality, asking for what you want
- **September:** Spring clean your mindset
- **October:** Halloween, horror stories, things that go wrong, fear of failure
- **November:** Celebrating success, reflect on the year
- **December:** Christmas stress, financial worries, nothing is perfect

Now use your brand One Word to create all of your marketing messages and set your themes for each month of the year. Once you have themes for each month you have a systematic approach for your marketing that ensures you are consistently out there with the right message at the right time.

This also means you can be flexible and responsive should something happen you haven't planned for. Rather than panicking each month to create something from nothing, you now have consistent marketing going out, and you can pick and choose to react to anything else.

You can download a Marketing Action Planner at
www.yourbrandtruenorth.com/MAP

Step 3: Write Blogs

Before you start writing your blog do your research. Discover the facts about events happening in each month you are writing for—anniversaries of world events, days of the year, celebrity birthdays. Research each theme and search the internet to discover the stories behind the topics or events that occur in each month. Consider the history behind global or annual events, check myths and legends, include celebrated days such as Halloween, April Fool's, or Valentine's Day to see if you have a story that relates to your brand strategy and can help reinforce your marketing messages.

Look into celebrity stories, historical information, or trends. Collect quotes, data, other news items for each theme. Consider a personal story or opinion about the theme that you can add, something political or environmental that is important to your audience, or discussed in popular culture. Find a storytelling angle that will build on your brand message just like we did with BBQ and Elon's Flamethrower.

You can use *www.daysoftheyear.com* and *www.thefamouspeople.com* plus lots of other websites to find interesting facts, special dates, and celebrity birthdays. Use these in your blog to increase the storytelling value in your content and give you lots of repurposing opportunities. (You will find out about *repurposing* next, in Step 4.)

Remember to relate your theme for the month back to your brand One Word and use those images, quotes, and relevant words in your treasure chest, to align each blog with your brand strategy.

Now that you have your themes and lots of content ideas it is time to create a blog. You want to write an article of somewhere between 300-1,000 words that is uploaded to your website. The whole purpose of this exercise is to give you marketing content that is easily repurposed to social media and so many other channels to drive traffic to your website. Once there, it is up to your website to convert suspects into prospects and prospects into customers.

Although you include content and links in your blog to any of the interesting details you have researched that fit with your brand theme and story, make sure the purpose of the blog is clear and presented in an appealing way.

A favourite blog format of mine is the 30/30/30/10 rule:

- **30 percent News**: The opening of your blog is the relevant information that gets someone reading it—data, stats, or an interesting story. Start with content that will create intrigue and get eyeballs on your blog. Consider what words the reader might use themselves that you can have in your opening statements. If you consider movie trailers as an example, they sell the sizzle not the sausage. This is how your blog should open, creating intrigue and being interesting enough to entice people to want to read more.

- **30 percent Information**: Now share some insight or opinion, maybe a few bullet points or one major lesson they can learn from you. This is your opportunity to show them your Expert-Ease, to share your ideas as a leader, and build your brand reputation as the #1 in your space. Giving away a bit of valuable, useful help or information tells your audience that you have more to offer and are worth following.

- **30 percent About**: This is where you can add a personal touch. Share how your business developed the solution to the problem you talked about at the start of the blog. It is here you can offer a service or product to help readers imagine the outcome you can deliver. You can highlight the business team or your innovation, give away a discount code or coupon, share a link to follow you on social media for more help, or simply suggest they share the article on their socials.

- **10 percent Fun and Inspiration**: Include images, memes, or quotes that reinforce your story and make them easy to share. Your blogs should make the reader feel something and encourage them to share the article just by having 'Tweetable' content.

Lastly, create a captivating headline that is short, catchy, and gives your audience a reason to click on it. Think about how well newspapers use headlines to captivate. You can test your headline on various sites including:

https://capitalizemytitle.com/headline-analyzer

If you don't like writing and this entire section has you sweating don't panic. Consider recording your voice and getting it transcribed. If you are not a natural writer you can create your themes and do the research and then get someone else to write the blogs. Just make sure they use a familiar tone of voice to you and words that fit with your brand personality.

You can always create vlogs (video blogs) instead of blogs, upload to your YouTube channel, or get them transcribed and turn them into a blog. There are so many great ways to create content now that you have your brand strategy and themes for each month. Now that you have awesome content, you need to make sure your audience sees it. It is pointless simply posting to your website and hoping people visit. You have to spread the word, so follow the paths on your MAP to get your message into the market.

Step 4: Repurpose

Now that you have a relevant and engaging blog on your website it is time to share it. The first share you can do is to your existing fans, emailing your database with a cut down version of the article and a link that sends them to your website where they might just find out more about you and your services or products.

Then you can share your blog on your social media channels. Sharing timely posts consistently on social media is great but the whole idea of being on social media is to entice your ideal clients to engage with you. The first step to do that is to have them click a link and come to your website to read your blog.

An SEO expert once told me that Google is like a river and all the fish swimming in it are your prospects. They need some bait in the water in order to come closer to your website, which is like a fish farm that is sitting on the bank of the river. When you share on social media it is like throwing chum into the water to entice the fish. If you pay for adverts on social media and online, that is like spearfishing your prospects. It is far more targeted and can land you a big fish, but costs each time you use it.

Organic marketing and paid advertising can work side-by-side, and you can use the same content and messages for both. You can also repurpose the same content across channels, including traditional media, direct marketing, and online.

The benefit of having blogs already written for each month is you can take excerpts and samples from them to create social media posts that are intriguing and entice your prospective clients to visit your site to "read more." If you have used images or quotes on your blog posts you can share them in your social media posts.

And here is the really cool part of having a Marketing Action Plan. You can use those special dates you researched and used in the creation of your blog during each month to repurpose and share your blog link. You can schedule social media around the details and facts you have included in your blog post. For example:

- March 11th is World Plumbing Day. Can you post about losing money 'down the drain?' That leads to a blog about financial advice.

- April 19th is World Bicycle Day. You could share a post about a health and wellbeing blog you have written.

- May 21st is World Hugging Day. Your blog post about being kind to your staff would be ideal to share on this day.

I bet you can find loads of these opportunities to repurpose your content. You can repurpose your blog in so many ways as well:

- One week you might schedule recording a video or go live on Facebook with a brief message that fits with your blog.

- You can create a LinkedIn event, hold webinars or Zoom calls to discuss the topic.

- The next week you might create an infographic, cartoon, or meme watermarked with your logo so if it gets shared, your brand does too. This is much better value that simply finding a nice quote with someone else's brand on it and sharing that.

- You can hold sales promotions or offers and giveaways all based on your monthly theme.

- You can apply to speak on podcasts and summits to share your expertise and your theme because it's current right now.

As a leader you can continue to get in front of the influencers, future partners, and employers with relevant content they will enjoy, remember, and share. You can be relevant and engaging, entertaining and interesting.

When you have completed your MAP with a theme for each month and key dates scheduled to share and repurpose the content, you can plan ahead and surround your audience with brand-focused content that amplifies what your brand stands for. Instead of reactionary or non-existent marketing, you now have everything planned for consistent activity each month.

Now you have the power of your brand compass keeping everything on track and a straight-forward path for the year ahead, with your MAP to follow.

Step 5: Repeat

Guess what? Now that you have your MAP and you are leveraging your brand message, you can simply repeat your activity the following year. You might want to update your blog posts to make sure they are current, but in reality you can repurpose each of the themes for the following year because the same things happen for your audience: Christmas, school holidays, end of financial year (EOFY). They occur each and every year.

All you have to do is stay consistent and be on-brand so that when your next prospect is ready for your help, they will find your marketing message and know you are the brand leader for them.

You now have everything you need to stand out as a leader, you just need to implement what you have learnt.

DO THE REPS

THE HOWLING BLAST of the wind is horrific as they slide open the door on the tiny aircraft that's been rapidly circling to 20,000 feet above Byron Bay. It's early in the morning on the 5th of October 2018, and I'm about to throw myself out of a perfectly good aeroplane to celebrate going 50 times around the sun. The adrenalin is already coursing through my veins and as my tandem skydiver edges closer to the open door my heart begins to race. For someone who is totally fearless it is this tiny moment, hanging on the outside of the plane and strapped to someone I now need to totally trust with my life, my stress level is elevated to its peak.

Time slows to a snail's pace in that split second between being in the plane and out of it. Suddenly we are falling towards the Earth. I gasp as the rush of the air distorts my cheeks and I'm very grateful for the plastic goggles shielding my eyes as we plummet at almost 200 km/h (120 mph), *straight down*.

After 60 seconds of freefall that feels like an age, the parachute opens and it is instantly quiet. We take in the beautiful view of the bay with the green and blue interchanging as we spiral slowly downwards.

Eventually we land and my friends who joined us for this exciting adventure are also coming back down to earth around me. Brightly-coloured chutes dot the field as we smile, hug, and high-five each other, whooping and laughing as the buzz from the jump continues.

Photos are taken and the champagne is popped while we enjoy birthday cake and more stories and laughs about our extreme morning. We return to the Airbnb for more fun, food, and celebrations that continue through the day and last long into the night.

Later when the excitement has worn off, I look at disgust at the photos of myself. Smiling and happy but obviously overweight. I struggle to deal with the fact that when we weighed in at the skydiving hanger that morning the scales revealed that I am almost 78 kg (172 pounds).

I face the reality. I am short, fat, fifty, unfit, and unhealthy.

I've always been a sporty person and competed in hockey, sailing, and swimming and of course still did bush walking. But years of having a sedentary job behind a computer and an ageing body that has had its fair share of health concerns have lead me to being the most unfit I have ever been.

By December I decide it is time to take action. Together with my husband we visit the local F45[78] studio that has just opened at the shopping centre down the road. We timidly venture up the stairs and cautiously open the glass doors to peer inside. At the desk a bubbly young lady with dark hair smiles broadly and says, "Hello!" but her welcome does little to reduce the anxiety we are feeling. We've never been gym bunnies, in fact I think I contracted Lyrca-phobia[79] when I spent a short time working as a step-aerobics instructor in the U.K. in the 90s.

We get a guided tour of the gym and are confronted by a room of people who look fitter than anything I've ever seen before. On the wall are giant TV screens with Cory G., the face of F45, in his light blue t-shirt, going through each of the exercises. A bright blue running track extends down the length of the room and that alone frightens me. I hate running. A timer goes off and

---

[78] F45 Training is a global fitness community specializing in innovative, high-intensity group workouts that are fast, fun, and results-driven. — https://f45training.com/

[79] Many of us can come up with a plethora of excuses to not visit the gym: We're too busy, too tired, membership is too expensive... But according to a new study, more than half of us avoid it for one main reason - Lycra. That stretchy, skin-tight, sometimes shiny fabric synonymous with active wear scares 51 per cent of Australians so much that they will skip working out publicly in order to avoid wearing it. —https://www.dailymail.co.uk/femail/article-3036360/The-biggest-cause-gym-phobia-revealed-51-cent-scared-work-public-look-LYCRA.html

everyone moves to the next station to keep going on their exercises.

Some of the movements I see I am certain I can never do. I'm far too old. I have too many aches and pains. *Holy moly,* I think to myself, *can we even do this?* Inside my brain a switch is flicked. I recall that image of me in the blue skydiving overalls and harness that pinches at the extra weight I am carrying, smiling at the camera from the adrenalin but looking puffy and tired.

We have to do something, we can't go on like this.

We sign up for a gym membership and as Jess cheerily waves us goodbye we promise to be there tomorrow morning for the 6 a.m. class. We do turn up the next day. And the next, and the next. Each morning at 6 a.m. we arrive, and we cautiously check the TV screens to see what Cory has in store for us. The trainers help us modify each station to suit what we can achieve. We do our first F45 Challenge and learn so much more about health, nutrition, and exercise than we ever thought we'd need to know.

I keep training at F45 and in the first challenge I reduce my fat by 12 kg. We complete six more F45 Challenges reducing my body fat percentage further each time and getting much, much fitter.

It's early morning again three years later when I wake and realise the day I've been working so hard to get to is finally here. Today however is something so far out of my comfort zone it frightens me even more than skydiving. Today is the ICN Sunshine Coast bodybuilding competition that my daughter, who is also competing, talked me into doing. We weigh in with our trainer and eat a tiny and very odd breakfast (30 grams of chicken, three rice cakes with jam, and 10 grams of dark chocolate), pack our bags, and leave the sanctity of our apartment for the local exhibition centre.

I am shaking like a leaf backstage as my coach helps me get pumped up for my first appearance.

As a keynote speaker I am most at home on stage, it's my happy place and I love it, but today I will be on stage wearing just a skimpy bikini, a tan, and my smile, *and it's freaking me out!*

My name is called and I step into the glare of the spotlights of the event centre. I weigh 54.4 kg (120 pounds) and my waist measures just 70 cm as I try to control my shaking when I go through the poses, smiling and looking the judges in the eye with as much confidence as I can summon.

The transformation for me to drop six dress sizes and rid my body of 23.6 kilos (52 pounds) in fat, getting my visceral fat (the dangerous stuff that lurks around your organs) from a rating of 12 to just 3, and to have less than 15 percent body fat, did not happen overnight.

It didn't happen in a couple of months or even a year.

It took three years of showing up, putting in the reps, and being prepared to listen, learn, and action what my coaches told me to do. Yes, it was hard. At times it was a total and complete challenge, but mostly it became an incredibly rewarding habit. I had amazing support around me and a goal to be fitter and healthier. I wanted to create a better me with the ability to leave a legacy, knowing I would be around for my family and I would be able to get more out of life as I aged.

Remember, owning a business and investing in being a stand-out leader is like buying a gym membership. If you don't show up, you don't get the results.

Your brand compass gives you the reason why you need to get out there and promote and market yourself and your business or services. But right now you need to take action and put in the effort to get your brand out there.

You have Your Brand True North to guide you and a MAP to follow. You know how to reach your ideal audience with the right message at the right time. It might be scary to get started, but you just need to put one foot in front of the other and take this one step at a time.

No matter what, if you want to be a stand-out leading brand you need to be consistent, to keep moving forward, to be accountable, and be your own best support team.

Being a leader can be lonely, so find others you can network with, support, and be accountable to as well. Join networks, attend events, find a mastermind group or a business buddy and report to each other.

You have invested in your brand so now put in the effort to climb that mountain and be the influencer at the summit of success that everyone looks up to.

YOU CAN DO THIS

WE ARE WALKING in the Hunua Ranges with a group of 50 kids and leaders. As usual Uncle George is way out in front, striding ahead up the narrow ridge that leads past the water catchment dam. After the hill climb we descend the ridge, heading down into the nīkau[80] grove that lines the base of the river. That's where we will stop for lunch and have a swim. The leader is one of the two most important people in the walking party and Uncle George certainly knows his way around the tracks, having lived in the area for years and walking hundreds of kilometres through the bush.

He knows all the native plants and often arrives home with saplings poking out the top of his backpack that he will nurture. They will get stronger until he can replant them back into the brush, where they will be able to grow into a giant totara[81] or mighty kauri[82] tree.

Yes, it is the leader that everyone looks up to and trusts that they know where they are going. But there is another vitally important person on any bush walk and they are right at the back.

---

[80] Rhopalostylis sapida, commonly known as nīkau (Māori: nīkau), is a palm tree endemic to New Zealand, and the only palm native to mainland New Zealand. Nīkau is a Māori word; in the closely related Eastern Polynesian languages of the tropical Pacific, it refers to the fronds or the midrib of the coconut palm. —https://en.wikipedia.org/wiki/Rhopalostylis_sapida

[81] Podocarpus totara (from the Maori-language tōtara; the spelling "totara" is also common in English) is a species of podocarp tree endemic to New Zealand. It grows throughout the North Island and northeastern South Island in lowland, montane and lower subalpine forest at elevations of up to 600 m. —https://en.wikipedia.org/wiki/Podocarpus_totara

[82] Agathis australis, commonly known by its Māori name kauri (pronounced "Ko-ree"), is a coniferous tree in the family Araucariaceae, found north of 38°S in the northern regions of New Zealand's North Island. —https://en.wikipedia.org/wiki/Agathis_australis

Tail-End Charlie

They are there to make sure no one falls behind or gets lost. It's their role to ensure the pace isn't too fast or too slow. They inform the leader if they are going too quickly or if they need to speed up to get everyone home on time. Mostly, Tail-End Charlie helps motivate the stragglers and keep the lollygaggers[83] in line.

As a leader we need to be our best supporter. We need to be our own Tail-End Charlie, making sure we are checking in with ourselves and avoiding getting distracted or diverting off the path.

We know success does not happen in a straight line. There are great days followed by dreadful days. Times we feel on top of the world, and days when we feel the world is out to beat us. As a leader with an entrepreneurial, superhuman brain, not only do you see lots of opportunities, you can also start to doubt yourself and your own abilities, especially as you grow and take on challenges while you step outside your comfort zone.

You may be at the end of this book thinking, *Wow this sounds awesome but I don't think I can do it.* You may think that branding and marketing is not in your wheelhouse, or that you still struggle to see yourself as a leader, especially if it's going to take so much time, hard work, and effort. You may worry you don't have the capability or creativeness to brand yourself, the confidence to push your message out there, or position yourself as the go-to expert.

Remember the Domino's Pizza delivery boy who came up with a billion-dollar brand name? When you are getting down on yourself and your capabilities just remember anyone can be creative. At times you may consider all of this branding and marketing might be too difficult for you, or that you're not clever or talented enough, or that you don't know enough or have enough experience or the right skills set. Perhaps you think you are not capable of being the leader your marketing is proclaiming

---

[83] lollygag: intransitive verb, to fool around and waste time :—
https://www.merriam-webster.com/dictionary/lollygag

you actually are. You may even worry that by standing out and being noticed you are being a fraud or an imposter.

All of these voices you hear inside your own head I call the 'Itty-Bitty-Shitty-Committee,' and you can definitely tell them, "Be quiet. Hold my beer, and watch me achieve success!"

Next time you hear them, think of all the amazing brands you have learnt about in this book and how they all started from nothing but a simple idea and grew because the brand developed meaning that matters to their raving fans.

Whenever you start to doubt your ability to be a great leader go back to Your Brand True NORTH and remember your purpose and passion.

Next time you worry you don't have anything of value, go back to EAST and know your Expert-Ease, or review how you transform lives in SOUTH, and all the people you can help in WEST.

You have the most amazing natural gifts that the world needs, and you deserve to be well-known, well-paid and wanted.

"A leader is one who knows the way,
goes the way, and shows the way."

~ John C. Maxwell

ACKNOWLEDGEMENTS

TEACHERS LEAD US through the formative years of life and I have Mr. Higgott, Mr. Rennie, and Mr. Wong to thank for the guidance they gave me to develop my skills as a dyslexic creative who loves a storytelling culture.

The creative industry is flooded with extraordinary talent, passion, and mind-blowing genius, and I have had the privilege of working alongside the most amazing teams with Chris Treseder at Shotz Reprographic; Doug, Catherine, and Noel at Ideas Advertising; Sarah Sortain-Smith at Clemenger BBDO; Nicholas Ward at Ogilvy & Mather; Kevin Roberts and Nicola Lowe at Saatchi & Saatchi; Michael Redman and Stewart Gilbride at Grey Worldwide; Gill Walker at Evergreen Marketing & Advertising; Ruth Colenso at AXA; and Annette Densham at the Audacious Agency who have all encouraged me to take a walk on the wild side of branding and step into the world of neurobranding.

As a keynote speaker my ability to share the stories behind brands has been amplified, thanks to the insight and education provided by Marty and Michael at MainStage, and to those who helped read through this book and provide feedback on the stories hidden in its pages. You have been instrumental in making everything flow. I am forever grateful for your assistance.

I would also like to thank all the professional conference organisers, associations, and franchises who have had me speak and share the brand stories that inspire and delight your audiences. Your confidence in me and the message I deliver is extraordinary, and I am so proud to stand on your stages.

I dedicate this book to my family: My mum and dad who taught me to believe in myself, my YMCA Camp family who gave me the confidence to step up and be a leader, my husband Graeme and my daughter Kerenza who continue to listen to my stories and laugh at my jokes no matter how regularly I tell them.

I also thank you, the reader, for taking the time to invest in your brand and for following me into the world inside your brain to discover purpose, meaning, and direction as a leader in business.

ABOUT THE AUTHOR

Growing up in the bush and being told as a child she had *word blindness* and wouldn't be able to read or write didn't stop Lauren going on to become a five-time bestselling author and multiple award-winner, using her dyslexia as her greatest asset, helping business leaders understand how the brain sees brands so they can navigate through a noisy and overwhelming world.

Lauren has worked at leading advertising agencies and in brand management for over 30 years, helping launch hundreds of global brands. She appears in worldwide media and on podcasts and summits as the sought-after personal branding specialist.

As a keynote speaker, The Brand Navigator, Lauren Clemett guides your audience, giving them a clear direction to communicate a consistent brand and marketing message, so they confidently take action as stand-out leaders in business. After hearing Lauren speak they will overcome overwhelm and lead with direction, purpose, and meaning, making marketing a walk in the park! Enquire today about Lauren's availability to speak at your next event:

www.yourbrandtruenorth.com

TAKE YOUR NEXT STEP!

CREATE YOUR MARKETING ACTION PLAN with a system to sustainably develop relevant content ideas and schedule social media, promotions, and meaningful marketing activity that keeps your brand in front of your audience all year round.

The Marketing Action Planner is the ideal companion to this guidebook and will help you implement what you have learnt and stay on track as a brand leader.

Get your own Marketing Action Planner:
*www.yourbrandtruenorth.com/*MAP

REFERENCES

[i] Business Failure Rate: https://www.fundera.com/blog/what-percentage-of-small-businesses-fail)

[ii] Business Marketing: https://nobullmarketing.com.au/small-business-marketing-survey-results-2020/

[iii] Content Created Each Day: https://seedscientific.com/how-much-data-is-created-every-day

[iv] Attention Span: https://time.com/3858309/attention-spans-goldfish/

[v] Website Traffic: https://www.marketingdive.com/news/google-53-of-mobile-users-abandon-sites-that-take-over-3-seconds-to-load/426070/

[vi] Lizard Brain: https://seths.blog/2010/01/quieting-the-lizard-brain/

[vii] Richard Branson Mr. Yes: https://www.cnbc.com/2017/12/18/billionaire-richard-branson-reveals-why-he-always-says-yes.html

[viii] Queen Elizabeth: https://www.nytimes.com/2012/06/03/fashion/queen-elizabeth-ii-sets-a-style-standard

[ix] Jeff Bezos: https://www.entrepreneur.com/article/379920

[x] DNA In Breath: https://respiratory-research.biomedcentral.com/articles/10.1186/1465-9921-10-86

[xi] Toblerone: https://www.mondelezinternational.com/Our-Brands/Toblerone

[xii] Human Signals: https://link.springer.com/referenceworkentry/10.1007/978-3-319-28099-8_707-1

[xiii] BIC Pens: https://www.thepenguy.com/bic-history

[xiv] Mark James, Dirty Bird: https://www.markjamesworks.com/about

[xv] Amazon: https://www.businessinsider.com/amazon-jeff-bezos-chose-company-name-2018

[xvi] WFI: https://www.wfi.com.au/about/history

[xvii] Audi: https://www.audi.com/en/company/history/history-of-the-logo.html

[xviii] Airbnb: https://blog.logomyway.com/airbnb-logo/

[xix] Westpac: http://overthenet.blogspot.com/2009/09/artists-in-ad-land-ralph-hotere.html

[xx] Dom Pierre Perignon: https://www.mashed.com/705353/how-champagne-was-accidentally-invented/

[xxi] Champagne: https://www.champagne.fr/en/comite-champagne/bureaus/bureaus/united-states/pages/protection-of-the-champagne-name

[xxii] Boost Juice: https://www.boostjuice.com.au/about-boost-juice/

[xxiii] Canva: https://www.forbes.com/sites/alexkonrad/2019/12/11/inside-canva-profitable-3-billion-startup-phenom/?sh=72c8be1e4a51

[xxiv] Michelin: https://bettermarketing.pub/the-greatest-logo-in-history-f33dcaacd455

[xxv] iPad: https://www.businessinsider.com/steve-jobs-threw-ipod-prototype-into-an-aquarium-to-prove-a-point-2014-11

[xxvi] Red Bull: https://www.redbull.com/au-en/energydrink/history-of-red-bull

[xxvii] Volvo: https://www.volvocars.com/intl/v/discover/heritage

[xxviii] Domino's: https://blog.logomyway.com/dominos-logo/

[xxix] Bobbi Brown: https://www.thefashionlaw.com/want-to-name-your-brand-after-yourself-think-again/

[xxx] McDonald's Founders: https://www.mashed.com/147897/the-tragic-real-life-story-of-the-mcdonald-brothers/

[xxxi] Heinz Sauce: https://www.bbc.com/news/business-34052147

[xxxii] Adidas: https://www.adidas-group.com/en/about/history/

[xxxiii] Coca-Cola: https://lemelson.mit.edu/resources/john-pemberton

xxxiv LEGO: https://www.lego.com/en-au/aboutus/lego-group/the-lego-group-history

xxxv Virgin: https://www.virgin.com/about-virgin/virgin-group

xxxvi Body Shop: https://www.thebodyshop.com/en-au/about-us/our-story/a/a00002

xxxvii DHL: https://www.dhl.com/au-en/home/press/press-archive/2021/dhl-express-australia-and-surf-life-saving-australia-extend-partnership-to-2024.html

xxxviii Red Bull Sponsorship: https://www.forbes.com/sites/jamesayles/2020/01/14/from-cliff-diving-to-formula-one-and-football-how-red-bull-built-a-world-class-sporting-empire/?sh=148ea0c0e1c1

xxxix Patagonia: https://allgoodtales.com/brand-story-hero-patagonia/

xl Elon Musk Flamethrowers: https://www.dailymail.co.uk/sciencetech/article-5843163/Elon-Musks-Boring-Company-flamethrowers-used-BBQ-meat-light-joints.html